P R

A PATH

SIGNS

AND SYN

C000135177

"Karen Tysver has been courageous enough to share with the reader her own intimate journey of discovery. She has allowed the images that emerged in her life to become symbols that reveal the unconscious aspects of her personality that need healing. She is diligent and tenacious in her attempt to awaken to her full potential. By experiencing her journey, the reader can be initiated into the process of becoming conscious through the symbols that appear in our lives. This is a powerful and much-needed work for our time."

~BETTY J. KOVACS, PHD

Author, *Merchants of Light: The Consciousness That Is Changing the World* and *The Miracle of Death: There Is Nothing But Life*

"Karen Tysver's book serves as a powerfully rich and compelling invitation for inner exploration, growth, and personal transformation! Using entertaining storytelling to reveal the everyday synchronicities and symbolism of our lives the reader will begin to look at their journey in an entirely new way, moving from a conditioned to a conscious life."

~ELISSA AL-CHOKHACHY, MA, BSN, RN

Author of *Miraculous Moments: True Stories Affirming That Life Goes ON*

A PATH TO
FREEDOM

SIGNS, SYMBOLS, AND SYNCHRONICITIES

KAREN TYSVER

Charleston, SC
www.PalmettoPublishing.com

A Path to Freedom

First Edition

Paperback ISBN: 979-8-8229-2939-5
eBook ISBN: 979-8-8229-1952-5

Introduction

I had absolutely no plans to write this book, a series of signs, symbols, and synchronicities led me here. A disembodied voice led me here.

A golden chain tree, known for their cascading chains of bright yellow flowers, grew in a park near my home. While out running errands, I thought of that tree and wondered how it was doing. I had never thought of that tree before. On the next trip to the park I checked on the tree and noticed that it had only a few leaves on one gnarled branch. I didn't give it a thought after that.

A few days later I heard a loud masculine disembodied voice say, "Golden Chain."

I shook my head, puzzled.

"Golden chain," the voice repeated.

Still puzzled.

"Golden chain. Google it," came next, with just a hint of exasperation.

So, I did as I was told and looked up golden chain. Apparently, disembodied voices tell you to do internet searches these days.

The first articles that came up in my online search of golden chain described it as a succession of teachers whose duty it is to keep the study and wisdom of symbolism alive to assist in the spiritual growth of humanity. Some of these sites simply had scanned pages of old documents referring to teachers of the Golden Chain. Others were more recent. I want to add that when I've gone back and done searches since then, none of these documents come up immediately. This information was the motivation the Universe provided me to write this book.

Carl Jung, the innovative psychoanalyst, recognized the power of using signs, symbols, and synchronicity in his personal life and when treating patients. I recently remembered a story in which he was deciding whether to take a trip quite far from his home. He was having a hard time weighing factors when he heard a tapping sound, looking up from his desk he saw a bird pecking at the window. He returned to his quandary, but the bird was incessantly clicking its beak on the pane of glass. It was a bird with which he wasn't familiar. With research, he found that it was native to the country he was considering visiting and not native to his home. With his belief in the ability of signs, symbols, and synchronicity to steer us in a helpful direction, he realized this was a clear sign to make the journey.

Some of the symbols we encounter may not be quite as straightforward in their direction and require help interpreting them. This book will guide you through some of the universal and very personal symbolism that appears in your life.

Upon receiving the symbolic, historical, and verbal messages about the golden chain I didn't immediately start to write this book. I avoided thinking about it due to a fear of failure, or perhaps a fear of success. Who knows what other fears may have been involved, but I put it off. *Fear is the Great Procrastinator.* When we are given directions through symbols and we don't follow them, we are given more signs with the same message. If we continue to ignore them, they become persistent and more obvious. To get your attention, these experiences may become painful, in physical, emotional, spiritual, or other ways.

This spring, about eight months after the first messages, I noticed that the one living branch on the golden chain tree in the park had some blossoms on it. I also realized from looking at the tree, that it wouldn't make it another year.

A few weeks later I saw that a gardener had planted a new golden chain tree next to the dying one, but part of the new tree's root ball was above the ground, and I knew it wouldn't survive. After a few days watching it slowly wither I was compelled to take a bucket of dark soil and my garden spade to the park. I dug up the young, dying tree, made a wider and deeper hole for it, re-planted it, and gave it a thorough watering. I returned daily to check on it. On the third day, I saw that the gardener had cut down the old Golden Chain tree and had inadvertently cut off the top of the new tree, ending any hope it would survive.

To me this was a clear message that I couldn't put off writing this book any longer. I needed to take my place as a member of the Golden Chain. If I put it off something even worse might happen to propel me into action. I didn't want to lose my head like the poor tree. I decided to go forth in faith that I would be led to everyone and everything I needed to complete the project. Each day I prefaced my writing by asking, "What would you have me say?" In this way I ensured the continuation of the golden chain with the help and blessings of guides and the teachers who had come before me. This insured I would write the book that jumped between the lines as well, surprising me with its message.

I hope that you find this book helpful, for symbolism can be used to answer questions both great and small. Never hesitate to ask for signs for you will be answered. Importantly, don't ignore what you're given. It's always better to get a tap on the shoulder than a hammer to the head.

Having said all that, it was not without trepidation that I commenced to write this book. This was a challenge, for I start many projects but finish few. Because of that pattern I have a long line of unfinished work behind me. Did I really want this to be another one? Who needs more shame? Deep down I knew that for my own well-being and spiritual growth I needed to show up for this project. I needed to commit and move forward. I needed to overcome the fear that often paralyzes me when starting projects. The symbolism of the golden chain tree dying and the new one being killed propelled me into action. Like many of my projects, the little golden chain tree was cut off before it had a chance to live. I couldn't let my fear stop me.

Death, in this case the death of a tree, is often symbolic of change and transformation. In all endings there is a new beginning. This new beginning for me was a deeper commitment to my spiritual growth and supporting the spiritual growth of humanity. I do not suppose that I have all the answers regarding the use of symbolism in everyday life. I am as much a student as a teacher. I showed up to write this book with the knowledge and trust I would be guided in its creation and people will show up to read it.

It is my belief that the same is happening to you—some unrecognized, or at best barely recognized, symbol is driving you forward—or you would not have picked up this book. Picking up this book is a sign that you are ready to "read" the signs, symbols, and synchronicities of your life. May it be the catalyst for you to realize the life you deserve.

Table of Contents

CHAPTER 1

Red Tailed Hawk

In a dream I was sitting in the luxurious dining car of an early twentieth century train. The dark woodwork glowed in the brilliant light pouring through the dining car's windows. White linens and polished silverware set the table. My traveling companions and I were enjoying a pleasant luncheon. Suddenly a Red-Tailed Hawk flew up alongside the window next to me. As I stared at the hawk, I could clearly see the finest detail of each feather and the black pupil in its golden eye staring back at me. It was compelling. The hawk continued to fly beside me and stare into my eyes. Then it looked down at my plate. My companions asked why it looked at my plate and I told them it was hungry. That was the entire dream. It was an incredibly vivid scene. I had the feeling of being bored while dining until the hawk flew up beside me and then it was as if I came alive, everything was more than it had been.

On a personal level, the Red-Tailed Hawk represents nature and freedom to me. For the past fifteen years or so I have taken a walk in the woods almost daily, weather not-withstanding. For about a week before this dream I hadn't walked in the woods.

The Japanese have a practice that is becoming more and more popular called Shinrin-Yoku; also known as forest bathing. The premise is that being in the resonance of nature for a few hours aligns us to our natural frequency and in doing so lowers our blood pressure, slows our heart rate, and increases our serotonin levels. Studies have confirmed the healing effects of this practice. The hawk was telling me that I needed some Shinrin-Yoku to nurture my body. The same resonance that lowers our blood pressure also quiets our mind. With a clear mind we can make better decisions and come to right choices more quickly than with a harried, anxious mind. The woods, the beach, the mountains all restore our emotional balance.

On a spiritual level symbolism has its highest meaning; let's explore the spiritual message of this dream. I was on a train. To me, any vehicle of transport represents our journey through life, our life's path or purpose. There are many idioms that support this symbolism: the highway of life, he was driven to succeed, she was on the fast track to success. How is a train different from other forms of transportation? A train is on a track and can only go in one direction. It is also used for mass transport.

A vehicle that carries many people often signifies going in the same direction as the society and culture into which we are born. This symbol told me I was following a path that conformed to my socioeconomic cultural group rather than pursuing a singular, self-fulfilling path. This track would represent the role assigned to me as a middle-class white female in America. What role were you assigned? Did the prevailing media messages influence your self-image as you grew into adulthood? Did you strongly identify with a specific social, cultural, or economic group? Was the education presented to you favorable and inclusive of your group and others? What were your expectations of what your life would be based on your childhood indoctrination? Did your parents have hopes for you that you may have internalized as yours? Are we programmed to grow up, go to college, get married, buy a house, have children, take yearly vacations, get promoted, save for retirement, move to Florida, and die? Did you just have an anxiety attack while reading that? Did you see the way we are conditioned when you read it? That scenario is proffered to us as the American Dream. If you live elsewhere, what dream does your country present to you? The world is so influenced by western media that this dream is becoming almost universal. Without the prescribed dream, what would we choose?

In my dream I was sitting in the dining car eating what was being offered to me. Food symbolizes nurturing. It is what feeds our body. As food nurtures our bodies so other aspects of our lives nurture our souls. This may symbolize that what I was feeding myself, my job, my leisure pursuits, my *thoughts*, my relationships, my *beliefs* were not feeding my soul. Even though there was food on my plate the hawk was hungry. The hawk, representing the part of me that wasn't being nurtured by my life choices, wanted something more, something unique to my soul. The hawk offered me freedom from the programmed beliefs of how my life should be. Staying on my prescribed, predictable *track* would never nurture or fulfill me. I was hungry for freedom. Freedom from the lie I was told as a child that I must conform, the lie that I wasn't worthy of a greater life. I was sitting in that dining car eating the bland food being offered me when right outside the window was complete freedom.

The hawk reminded me that I wasn't being creative and uniquely me. I was living unconsciously, following the track prescribed by my conditioning. We thrive when we have enthusiasm for our goals. The hawk wanted me to nurture my creative soul.

What other significance might the hawk have? We can ask questions to help us see the full meaning of symbols. Are there any special traits about the hawk that stand out to you? Do you experience a certain feeling when you see a hawk soaring above? I know that hawks fly higher than any other bird. To me, this would signify letting go of earthly limitations. Earthly limitations would include roles based in the collective conditioning of our demographic. We are not a demographic; we are individuals. Flying above all the rest, the hawk sees all the possibilities and potential. To me, this signifies that once we let go of limiting programming, we will see that we are capable of things we can't even imagine from our current conditioned vantage point. The hawk tells me to expand my vision for my life and go beyond any indoctrination I have that is holding me back.

What about the people with me? I would call them benign. They could have been anyone, but in the dream they represent me. This tells me that I was living a benign life, a mediocre life, nothing special, nothing inspiring, stimulating, or individuated. Though my companions weren't harmful or aggressive, there was no challenge, no excitement, no flourishing interest, no inspiring conversation. This dream was telling me that I was not any different than the millions that ride the figurative train every morning to their cookie cutter jobs and at the end of each day ride back to their cookie cutter homes, teaching their children to grow up and take the same track they did. This is how I was raised. My fellow passengers represented me, the average person who doesn't question their belief system, living the average life that was prescribed by society. I was the programmed passenger striving to fit in and prove how perfectly normal I was.

The train car was luxurious. We are taught the American Dream leads to wealth. We can have the material things we want. The question is, does that track lead us to a life fulfilled? I had luxury at my fingertips, but I wasn't thriving on that train. I was bored until the hawk showed up, I was practically asleep, unconscious. Then, when the hawk flew up to the window, I suddenly felt alive and invigorated. I don't want a safe perch; I want unlimited heights. I want a life unique to what I am, not the role I was assigned as a child. We are referred to as consumers. Most accept this moniker without any question. Are you a consumer or a Creator?

Do you identify yourself as part of an index measuring how you contribute to society by buying stuff? I would rather we have a happiness index, a compassion index, or a love index.

In the dream I was going in the same direction as everyone else because when you're on a train you have no choice. In life, *we have a choice*. We must try not to get caught up in the expectations of our *station* in life, in the labels we adopt. Are you courageous enough to color outside the lines? I would rather be labeled quirky, eccentric, or unique than a consumer.

One of the scariest unconscious beliefs we have as children is that if we do not conform to our parent's expectations they will abandon us. Our amygdala, the primitive instinctual part of our brain, flies into adrenalin mode when our parents are angry at or disappointed in us. In primitive human society if a child was abandoned it would, quite literally, die. When our parents disapproved of some behavior or aspect of us, we suppressed our emotions to please them, we denied our joy, put aside our desires, and killed our dreams for their approval. We adopted a construct given to us by our parents of how our lives should be. We accepted this construct because of a primitive, instinctual drive to survive because the amygdala told us we needed our parents to keep us alive. As adults we can override the archaic messages of the amygdala.

If we suppressed our emotions, our desires, our true nature as a child in an unconscious and often irrational primal fear that our parents would abandon us, or in the more reasonable ego fear that they would withhold love, punish, or deny us, we now have the exciting opportunity to discover our true nature and live our authentic life. We may have no memories of our parents or society directing our life, but we have internalized these constructs nonetheless and our lives reflect that.

The hawk was crying out to me, asking me what I was doing. Did I think that I had no option but to be on the same track as everyone else? We need to listen to our hearts and make decisions that are based on what we love, based in our intuition, our Highest Self.

To be true to oneself one must give up every belief formed without conscious analysis. This includes virtually every belief we hold because these beliefs were imprinted on us in childhood and reinforced as we grew older. We were told who we were before we had a chance to allow our authentic selves to emerge. We buried our desires, in fact our very self, every time we were told no, every time we were told to behave in a certain way, to believe a specific ideal, or to follow the path travelled by our cultural group. We bury our desires so deeply that it takes a long time before we realize why we are not happy. We can reclaim ourselves when we let go of who we are not. Just knowing that we have unconscious beliefs is the first step in rewriting the Story of Our Life.

We are far more than the erroneous beliefs taught to us as children. Our True Self is eternal and powerful beyond our imagining. Let go of beliefs that you are unworthy because of your gender, sexuality, financial status, clothing, car, education, religion, ethnic group, skin color, face, or body image. None of these beliefs have any basis in a Truth that is Eternal.

The hawk was telling me to get off the track that everyone else was on and find universal, infinite truths; truths that feed my soul and open me to Higher Consciousness, not temporary facts that make me fear not fitting in, not being good enough, and not being normal.

The day I woke up from this dream I followed one of the messages and took a walk in the woods. I found a Red-Tailed Hawk feather on my path. We will often experience synchronicities like this as validation of a message from our Higher Self. If you receive a second and even a third synchronistic sign or symbol with the same message, take a closer look, can you take the interpretation to a deeper level? Can you start to make the changes that the symbolic messages are asking of you? Until you start listening and acting on the advice from your Higher Self, you will remain stagnant, and harder messages will be delivered. These messages are a gift. Accept them and follow their wisdom.

For now, let's be mindful of negative thoughts and beliefs about ourselves, they are the voice of our childhood authorities. Observe the thoughts without judgment. The Buddhists call this the watcher, some call it witnessing our thoughts. When consciously witnessing our thoughts, we may notice that we are imagining ourselves failing at something, thinking of everything that could go wrong, telling ourselves we can't do it, or talking to ourselves in a way that we would never talk to a friend. Don't judge yourself for the negative self-talk, it's simply a recording of your programming being played by the ego. Applaud yourself for recognizing negative thoughts and stopping them. Negative self-talk is a habitual mind pattern. You can overcome your habit of negative thinking with practice.

Daily I am going to remind myself that I can make choices without limiting myself with indoctrinated beliefs. I am not who I was told I was, I am far more than that and so are you.

What were you told your role was? When you tried to express your true nature were you thwarted? Do you feel fulfilled in your life? Do you feel like you are making life decisions or are you on autopilot? Why did you choose your career? What does a hawk signify to you? Do you have a personal interpretation of a train, of food, of wealth? What excites you and nourishes your soul?

CHAPTER 2

Making All Things New

C hildren don't have the discernment of mature adults. They internalize the words and actions they experience. They don't consider that the adult influencing them may be fallible. My seven-year-old granddaughter knew something she told me was undoubtedly true because the smartest person in the world told her, "My teacher."

What if my granddaughter's teacher told her something about herself that wasn't true? Since her teacher is the smartest person in the world my granddaughter would hold her opinion as fact. What if she gave her a look that told her what she was doing was "bad?" She might internalize that coloring outside the lines wasn't acceptable and, by extension, she wasn't acceptable. What if her teacher made a comment on her spelling test that made my granddaughter feel she wasn't smart enough? What if this authority figure said something mean to her or to another child that my granddaughter witnessed? My granddaughter would place great store on anything the "smartest person in the world" said or did. As an adult my granddaughter may not remember specific experiences, but subconscious beliefs have been instilled in her. It is now part of her identity.

Your father may have asked you as a child what was wrong with you when you did something he found unreasonable, or you didn't know something he thought was universal. You may have internalized the message there was something wrong with you, but you didn't know what. This may have brought into conception the idea there were things everyone knew to which you were not privy. Why don't I get it? What's wrong with me? How can a child possibly know something they haven't been taught? Even so, the perception you are uninformed, out of the loop, and stupid was born.

We might forget the initial experiences that led us to question our worthiness or competence, but we are left with a belief something is wrong with us. We spend our life trying to be like everyone else so no one will find out that in some indelible way we are wrong. If we do remember experiences in which we felt bad about ourselves we often negate the impact they had, and still have, on our self-perception. Or we may adopt a victim role. We tell ourselves the story of our mistreatment over and over. Victim becomes our identity. We get attention when we are a victim. We feel superior to the mean people.

Your father may have praised you for your athletic ability and, enjoying his approval, you internalized the notion being an athlete was a positive thing for you. You believed if you continued as an athlete people would like you and admire you. It became part of your identity. I am an athlete therefore I am acceptable and worthy. I have importance. What happens if you get injured? What is your identity then? An arguably more important issue, what is your true passion? Is there another path which might have better filled you with a passionate enthusiasm? Have you neglected interests that appealed to you because you internalized the belief that being an athlete was the best path for you? Is your life unexplored because you labeled yourself an athlete, *or any other role assigned to you*, due to the subconscious need for the approval of an authority figure or peer?

Perhaps all you seemed to hear as a child was that money doesn't grow on trees, you can't have that, it's too expensive, you must work hard to get anywhere, the rich get richer, etc. You internalize the belief that money will always be a struggle and that you are not worthy of material riches.

Your teacher didn't understand how you processed information and labeled you an inadequate student. She didn't know that you were highly intelligent and could, in other circumstances and with a different teaching method, blow her away in intellectual pursuits, but you believed what she said and stopped trying. Due to her uninformed opinion, you adopted the belief that you are intellectually inferior.

Your grandmother told you that you were plain. You believed her and didn't see the beauty of your infectious smile and bright, laughing eyes.

Our history books told us our country (no matter what country) was the best and indoctrinated us to idealize our nation and its symbols regardless of the actions of the government. They told us that if we don't support our leaders blindly, we aren't patriots. And so, we accepted this as true and see our country through the mark of the victor's pen.

Our religion taught us we are sinful and shameful. It taught us we need to repent; we should be ashamed, we need to suffer to earn God's love. Lord, I am not worthy.

Source, the Universe, is trying to awaken us through signs, symbols, and synchronicities to show us who we truly are. It wants to shine a light on the erroneous beliefs we learned so we can discard them and discover ourselves.

The question we must ask is "How did I come to be who I *think* I am?" If we are not the author of our beliefs, how can we be the author of our own unique and magnificent life? How can we write the true story of our life if it is based on false premises? Without reviewing and examining our beliefs we will be doomed to an unintentional life, an unexamined life, casualties of our conditioning. It's time to take off the masks put on us by society.

By letting go of the programming we can reclaim who we are. We can let go of behaviors that undermine our progress. We can discard old limiting beliefs. We can create a conscious life of purpose. We can *create* our own unique identity.

Don't give your power to a set of beliefs instilled in you before the age of reason, before you were able to understand exactly who you are. There is no perfect being on earth. We are all flawed. If you received your beliefs about yourself from flawed individuals, you can be sure they're not going to serve you well. Try as our childhood authorities might, they couldn't give us what we needed to feel fully loved.

The Truth is there is no one on earth better than you are. And no one worse than you. The Truth is you are valuable, worthy, deserving, and lovable just as you are. You are good enough. Once you have the ability, and it's not hard, to recognize the messages the Higher Self is sending you through signs, symbols, and synchronicities, your life will change.

Our indoctrinated responses come as naturally as breathing. We want to stop that unconscious way of living, which brings us the same issues we've always had in relationships, career, finances, life. We can go through our entire lives making choices based on our programming. Once we recognize we have ingrained beliefs we can start to question them. We can't begin to grow until we realize we have been programmed in the same way a computer is programmed. Our actions are based on this software. It is liberating to be able to make choices based in truth and not on the erroneous constructs we internalized as children.

We are all part of the Universal Consciousness. We receive personal messages from it, to help guide us in our decision making and awaken us to our potential. This Source Consciousness is what sent me the signs, symbols, and synchronicities of the Golden Chain and led me to write this book.

The messages Source Consciousness sends us are like subliminal messages in the media; they happen all the time, but we are usually unaware of them. Just as a cymbal is used in an orchestra to emphasize the highest point of the piece, symbols are sent by the universe to awaken us to our highest good. Have you ever seen a humor piece in which someone crashes cymbals together to wake someone up from a sound sleep? Symbols are here to wake you up from your subconscious beliefs.

Universal Consciousness can be compared to a vast library that holds every thought, every word, every idea, everything ever created or that will be created. It is outside the constructs of time and space. It is a shared mind. Some call it the Higher Self, and you are a part of it. Some call it the One Intelligence, the One Truth, the Universe, the Collective Consciousness, the Holy Spirit, the Source, or God. It goes by many names. Use whatever term feels most comfortable to you. If you don't believe in any of it, just open to the possibility that there is more to life than you can imagine. Just consider it. Suspend your disbelief for a little while. It can't hurt.

Symbols come to us in different forms, through the physical world, through our dreams, through our thoughts, and through our emotions and desires. No one form of symbolism is more important than another, though repeated symbols, synchronicities, are pushing us to pay attention.

Our goal is to move from living an unconscious life based on our conditioning to a conscious life based in the Truth of who and what we are.

CHAPTER 3

Dolphins

A Dream: My brother, Sam, and I were swimming effortlessly underwater in a deep, wide river. The water grass gently swayed in the current. Coming upon a pod of pure white dolphins we swam along with them. They were very playful and seemed to enjoy being with us. It felt wonderful to swim with them, to be so free and joyfully alive.

Without warning my brother took a knife from his belt and stabbed one of the dolphins. The water turned red with blood. Without using words, I let my brother know that he couldn't do that. He was surprised that I was upset. Even though he appeared to have no comprehension that what he had done was wrong, he somehow understood that he couldn't kill them because they were perfection. End of dream.

I had this dream decades ago. Apparently, it stuck with me. A general rule in interpreting dreams is that any people or animals in your dream are aspects of your personality or psyche. We were quite young in this dream. I had the dream in my twenties, but felt we were approximately eight and ten in this dream, he being my older brother.

Sam was angry as a child. Our father wanted to mold Sam into someone my brother was not. He didn't respect Sam's right to be himself. Sam was forced to do what my father wanted; his anger was a reflection of his frustration.

In this dream I can easily venture to guess that my brother represented the aspect of my personality that held anger towards our father. My father was Sicilian and often in that culture girls are considered second-class citizens. I was unimportant to my father.

My younger brother, Greg, and I were born on the same day, five years apart. One year, on our birthday, Greg and I were sitting on the couch when my father got home from work. He said happy birthday to my brother but had completely forgotten that it was also my birthday. How can a parent who has two children born on the same day forget one of their birthdays? This behavior and similar by my father cemented my belief that I was invisible, unimportant, and unworthy. It's fair to say I had a few anger issues concerning my father at the time I had this dream.

Let's ask some questions about my dream. What do dolphins represent? I looked at some of the traits of dolphins. There are countless documented stories of dolphins rescuing people. A man having a heart attack while swimming was kept afloat by a dolphin until his mates on the boat saw him and were able to pull him aboard. A family of four on vacation was taking a swim when they were herded tightly together and surrounded by a pod of dolphins that circled around them for an hour until the great white shark lurking nearby swam off. At first the father, not aware of the great white, thought the dolphins were just playing and started to swim away, but one of the larger dolphins blocked him and nudged him back to safety.

Dolphins use sonar to "see." Sonar waves emit from their forehead and bounce back to them when they are blocked by an object, their brain interprets the returning data. Everything in the dolphin's path is "seen" through vibration in this way.

Dolphins in the wild are well known for being fun loving and enjoying life. They are considered the only mammal, besides humans, who have sex just for fun. They play games with each other. They surf the wakes of boats; they leap and dance for no reason other than the joy of it. They are as curious about humans as we are about them, often showing up at beaches to people watch.

The word dolphin comes from the Greek word for womb. Until the early 1800's dolphins were thought to be fish. Once they were known to have live births, they were named the equivalent of "fish with womb." For me their name carries strong symbolism for the Divine Feminine, nurturing, and creativity because their name includes womb. What is more creative than a womb, what is more nurturing?

The dolphins in the dream were white. What does white symbolize in our society or to you personally? For me it represents innocence, purity, spiritual wisdom, and healing.

In this dream my brother represented a part of me. My brother was very surprised when I told him he shouldn't kill the dolphin. He didn't see anything wrong with it. This tells me that at the time of the dream I was oblivious to the fact that my anger was hurting me. The Universe was trying to get me to recognize through symbols how harmful my anger was so that I could deal with it in a healthy way.

In essence, and quite simply, the dream was telling me that the angry part of me (my brother in the dream) would kill everything good in my life (the dolphin part of me). It would kill my chance for happiness, joy, and playfulness. It would kill my innocence, turning it into bitterness. The red blood draining from the dolphin would represent the draining of my joy. Our blood brings oxygen to our cells, it allows our breath, our life force to reach every cell of our body. Without it we die. If we have a blood defect we become fatigued, pale, weak, we can't run, play, or function. All things being equal, our blood, when it is healthy and able to transport oxygen and other nutrients, allows us to enjoy life without limits, to completely embrace our full capacity.

The dolphin's wound represents the fact that my anger hurts only me. I need not accept my father's treatment of me as a personal attack. His belief in the low status of girls and women resulted from his indoctrination and conditioning. It is not a reflection of who I am, my importance or worthiness. In the dream the dolphin didn't attack after being attacked. It gracefully swam off. I can swim away from all of it. I can forgive and free myself from anger and resentment.

The sonar of dolphins is very significant. To me it represents our third eye chakra. Chakras are energy centers in our body. Our third eye chakra is located behind and slightly above our physical eyes. Just as the vibration of the dolphin's sonar emits through its forehead, our third eye can reach a vibration through which we can clearly experience Source Energy, Love. The third eye represents our spiritual sight.

Imagine a bottlenose dolphin and their high forehead. There is literally a measurable vibration emitting from their foreheads. I would be curious to see the results of a study done of the third eye of humans. Do we emit a frequency, can it be qualified and quantified? I think it can. This symbolism is telling me that I will never experience spiritual enlightenment in a vibration of anger. The vibration of Love is the only way to Source. Love and anger can't coexist. My anger was preventing me from accessing and developing my third eye.

The ocean is often referred to by scientists as the Primordial Soup, all life on earth originated in the ocean. It is symbolic of the *Creative Source Energy*, God; use whatever word feels non-triggering to you. The ocean represents infinity, things hidden, such as those things we can't perceive with our five senses. There are still parts of our oceans that are a complete mystery to us. So much of Creative Source Energy is still unknown to most of us. The river leads to the ocean, so in the dream it represents my path to God, to Eternity.

I wrote that I told my brother without words that he couldn't kill the dolphins. To me this means that our highest expression is not through language but through vibration. *When we are vibrating at the frequency of Love our actions reflect our high vibration.* Intuition is part of our vibration. If I listened to my intuition I would experience a better life free from resentment and blame.

Anger vibrates at a very low frequency; joy at a high frequency and they can't coexist.

This dream clearly showed me the consequences of choosing anger over forgiveness and love. I choose to see my father's treatment of me simply as his indoctrination. It has absolutely nothing to do with me. It didn't even have anything to do with him. He was living out his programming. He was enmeshed in ego. He had no mind of his own. Why would I take it personally? I choose joy and playfulness over anger.

~

When my younger daughter was fifteen, we took a trip to Mexico. More than anything else she wanted to swim with the dolphins. Knowing what I now know I would never have supported the captivity of any living being. We arrived at the dolphin facility and were brought to an enormous swimming pool. There were twelve people. Four dolphins swam in the pool. We were instructed to sit on the edge of the pool while the dolphins circled the pool. One of the dolphins stopped every time she got in front of me and stared at me for a few seconds. My daughter asked me why the dolphin kept looking at me, but I didn't have an answer.

We were told to swim into the pool and the dolphins would swim around with us. Once near the center of the pool the dolphins surrounded me, covering me from head to toe, gliding against me in the water, encircling me. I was completely surprised and amazed. They wanted to make physical contact with me, to touch me. It was such a unique joyful experience that I find it hard to describe. After a minute or so my daughter broke the spell by yelling, "Mom, let the other people play with the dolphins, too!" I told her that I wasn't doing anything, it was the dolphins.

What an experience. I was immersed in my spiritual life (water) at that time, meditating and practicing yoga daily focusing on the Divine (third eye), mindful of my thoughts and energy. I was in the middle of a creative writing project (divine feminine, womb). I was practicing seeing the world and all that was in it through the eyes of the Christ Consciousness, of Love (high vibration). The only explanation I can come up with is that the dolphins, being an animal of vibration, picked up on my energy and it was a vibrational match. We were immersed with each other's frequency for a short time, and it was quite magical. This event validated the work I was doing on my spiritual path. It reminded me that my path was destined to bring me great joy, as it did on that day.

∼

Many years earlier, at seventeen, I left home and college and took an extended trip to Florida. I was visiting an outdoor dolphin habitat, a contained ocean inlet. The group that I entered with, led by a dolphin trainer, walked along wooden piers over the water. The trainer was having the dolphins perform for us but one of the dolphins wouldn't retrieve a plastic ring. The trainer gave up trying to get the dolphin to comply and led everyone away. I was the last one in line when the dolphin retrieved the ring and brought it to me. She was insistently nodding her head for me to take it, so I took it.

The trainer saw the interaction and scolded me for taking the ring because he said it would interfere with their training.

What is the symbolism here? The dolphin was offering me a gift. Now, knowing the wonderful symbolism of the dolphin, I think it was offering me a life filled with fun, joy, and spiritual fulfillment. I was being told that this life is available to us all.

We create our own life. We are the writer, producer, director, even the actors of our personal story. Everything in our life, every little thing that happens or that we see before us we have created with our beliefs. This incident was a very telling *projection of my belief system in that moment.*

Let's decipher this situation with the dolphin and trainer. Look at what the dolphin was offering me. It was a ring. A ring is a circle. A circle holds everything within it. It is whole. A ring is also a vibration, as in the sound emitted by a bell. A bell ringing in a church tower calls us to spiritual practice, a phone ringing tells us someone wants to communicate with us. On a spiritual level the dolphin was offering me everything, the gifts of Spirit, eternity, infinity, unlimited energetic power, Oneness in communion with the Divine. On a physical level it was offering me abundance, the whole world. On an emotional level it was offering me connection, happiness, and deep bonds with others. A circle of friends, an energetic bond, a vibrational match. I accepted that gift for one delightful moment. My Higher Self accepted the gift. The part of me that knows my worth accepted the gift. It was the gift of a joyful life.

It didn't last long before the trainer (representing the ego self, the conditioned self) reminded me that I wasn't worthy of such a gift, the gift of an incredible, magical life. The trainer scolded me for taking the gift. He was saying to me, "That's not for you, who do you think you are, you don't deserve such a fine gift, a gift from the Universe. A gift like that is for worthy people, people who matter." How could I have forgotten for even a moment that I was unworthy of such a life? I certainly couldn't accept such a life. That life was not for me but for someone who was important. I hung my head in shame.

The trainer said that I was interfering with the dolphin's training. Symbolically, to me, he may as well have been saying that I was messing up the programming, the conditioning, the indoctrination of the dolphin. The dolphin, representing another part of me, wanted to do something outside of its programming, it wanted to go into Source vibration (the ring) and be its Higher Self, but the trainer (acting as the programmed ego) was thwarting any attempts it made to become liberated. I had left college and the indoctrinated life and basically run away from it. Perhaps my intuition kicked in and said Run! Maybe my Higher Self was warning me not to step into the trap of prescribed adult roles.

The Dolphin, representing the part of me that knows what I am, an integral part of the One Consciousness, was offering me the world. The trainer (the ego, conditioned to believe I am unworthy) reminded me of how insignificant I was compared to others. Isn't it terrible how erroneous beliefs that we accept as children affect our entire lives until we recognize and deal with them? Is this how you talk to yourself or see yourself? I wish I had known about personal symbolism then!

Don't perpetuate the lies of fear. Accept the gifts offered to you daily by your Higher Self, by the Christ Consciousness that you are. Allow yourself to believe in your inherent and unconditional worthiness.

Affirmations can be helpful *when we claim their Truth*. I accept my worthiness. I accept a life of abundance and joy, of love and light. I accept the guidance of my Higher Self that knows who I am, a Limitless Being. I am a being of Perfect Potential.

What do you think of when you think of dolphins? Perhaps you have a very different view of them than I. Do you see them as happy and playful? Why would blood represent joy? Can you think of any idioms that describe blood that way? Clearly blood represents life, without it there is none. The dolphin's echo location center is in the same place as our third eye. If you meditate, touch the third eye location when you start and center your attention there. Not every time, just occasionally. Can you feel a vibration there or a density? Both are positive.

There aren't many negative attributes to Dolphin symbolism. The biggest thing to be aware of if you feel you've had a negative dolphin dream or experience is to not be too much of a rescuer. You don't want to lose yourself in everyone else's needs. In ancient Greece the symbol of two dolphins represented balance. We can use discernment in our rescuing behaviors.

CHAPTER 4

Merry Christ Consciousness

I had this dream many years ago and it is still one of my favorites. I was at a beach with a large walkway above it. A crowd was milling above the beach, chatting with each other. I was in that crowd. On the beach I saw two or three people testing the water, sticking their toes in, no one in above their ankles. On the sand, half a dozen people looked at the shoreline trying to decide if they wanted to go in.

In the crowd I ran into my old friend, Tim. I was ecstatic to see him. "Where have you been!" I cried. He looked at me, obviously a little puzzled, "I've always been here," he replied. End of dream.

When there is a person you know in one of your dreams the first question to ask yourself is what that person means to you. A brief description without giving it too much thought usually suffices. Normally I would have said that Tim was a kind, playful man, easy to laugh, but the first fact that popped into my head was that he was born on Christmas day. So, what part of me did Tim represent in this dream? My first thought was the birth of Christ, Christ Consciousness, the awakening of Spirit.

This dream reminded me that the Christ Consciousness is a part of me. I asked the Christ Consciousness (Tim in the dream) where it had been, and it told me that it was always with me. In my dream I was reminded that the Christ Consciousness is not something I am striving to attain, it is what I am, it is my being, it has always been here within me waiting for me to accept it, to have full trust in it, and to allow it to express in my life. It is a dream of self-realization.

In the dream I was not in the ocean (God) but milling around with the crowd. At that time in my life, I had forgotten who I was. The people on the beach (also me) were ready to examine their spirituality (ocean). They were exploring, testing the waters. The people above the beach were mindlessly wandering, not knowing where they were going, unaware of who or why they were. They also represented me. Their mindless, superficial chattering was symbolic of the mindless thoughts constantly distracting me from what is important.

Tim reminded me that he (the Christ) has always been here with me. To me, the Christ Consciousness is the energy of the Divine, of Infinite Love, of Eternal Truth, of Endless Joy, of Absolute Abundance. The Christ Consciousness is All That Is, All That Was, and All That Will Be. It is Source Energy. What a wonderful reminder of who I am.

~

The day after I wrote about my dream of Tim, I ended up behind the real Tim in line to get into the town dump. What a synchronicity! Since I was in my car that would symbolize my path in life. It seems I was doing better following (being behind Tim) my Christ Consciousness. I'm following Jesus to the dump! What could this mean? What do you think it means? What questions would you ask here? Why was I on my way to the dump? To me it says I am letting go of that which no longer serves me. I am getting rid of the trash, my false beliefs. I'm dumping them. Christ is leading me to the dump to release lies. Now I'm ready to fill my life with Eternal Truth.

I have asked for help from my Higher Self in letting go of old beliefs and hurts. I have asked for help to forgive so I no longer hold my fellow humans in judgment, whether it's their appearance, their actions, their words, or their beliefs upon which I place judgment. I am asking for help in letting go of anger and resentment. I am asking for help letting go of what no longer serves my soul or the Higher Good. I'll follow Christ to the dump any day!

This is a good visualization tool. Imagine yourself in your car, bringing your erroneous beliefs to the dump. Throw every self-doubt, every self-condemnation, every self-deprecation, every negative self-belief you have about yourself into a dumpster. Throw your shame into that dumpster where it belongs. Throw your anger and resentments in. Unload that car. Throw away everything anyone ever told you that you are. Throw away your mistaken identity. After you are done imagine a beautiful light surrounding all of it, the Light of Truth. All those lies, mistakes, beliefs, and unconscious agreements dissolve into the beautiful light never to bother you again. Or you could start a dumpster fire. Whatever works for you. Now, drive away. Experience your freedom! From now on only you will decide who you are, based in Truth. What a relief!

~

I saw Tim again about a month later. I was at the local hardware store where he works. As I was in the parking lot leaving the store, I saw Tim talking with a customer. We greeted each other and as I was loading my car, I heard Tim tell the man that he and I used to be roommates.

"Oh, really," said the man, "when was that?"

"In the hospital," Tim replied.

"Wait, that's not true, they don't allow men and women to share rooms in the hospital," the man said.

"Sure they do." I answered.

"Absolutely," said Tim.

"When was that?" asked the man.

"1954." I said.

"Ohhhhhh," the man laughed, "when you were born."

"Yeah," said Tim, "I had to stay at the hospital because everyone in my family was sick. I was there for two weeks before I could go home."

"And," I said, "I was born five days after Tim."

In my dream when I asked Tim, who represented Christ to me, where he had been, he responded, "I've always been with you." This encounter, another beautiful synchronicity, reminded me that quite literally, in this lifetime, Tim has always been with me. He was there at my birth. What an incredible reminder of the fact that Christ Consciousness exists in me and I in it and it always has and always will. Christ Consciousness is my frequency. It is the vibration in which I live.

I always knew the story of Tim and our first "meeting," but I didn't think about the symbolism of our being in the neonatal nursery together as it related to the dream and to my life. What better sign for me that I am and always have been with God, in God, and of God.

Can you imagine yourself as a newborn? Imagine a beautiful golden light of God's Love surrounding you. That light still surrounds you; you are immersed in God's Love. Truly, God has always been with you. You are one with God. You are Divine.

CHAPTER 5

We're all Animals

Animals seem to frequently factor into symbolic messages. I believe this is because they have distinctive characteristics. We automatically have specific thoughts about many animals. When you think of a tiger what comes to mind? I think about the fact that they are often considered the world's apex predator. A horse? A whale? They each represent distinctive traits or qualities to us. If an animal factors into a symbolic message to you, consider how that trait pertains to you. Do you share that characteristic? Do you consider it negative or positive? Is it absent in your personality or too pronounced? Does the animal have some positive traits and some negative traits?

Let's look at hummingbirds as an example of how to establish the symbolism of an animal. Imagine that suddenly you are seeing hummingbirds everywhere. Synchronicities like this are a message asking you to explore further. The first questions I would ask to help me decipher hummingbird's symbolism are: What do I think of when I think of hummingbirds? What does a hummingbird do? How do they make me feel? Examine your answers for an idea of their personal symbolism for you.

Here are some of my thoughts. You may have very different views about hummingbirds. Hummingbirds flit from flower to flower at an incredible speed, they beat their wings at an incredible speed, they do everything at warp drive. If you're seeing hummingbirds when you usually don't you might want to look at whether you are rushing around too much, running from one task to the next, not taking any time to just relax. Are you doing a million things at once? Are you burning yourself out?

If you find this answer resonates with you the next step is to discover why you feel a need to push yourself to the limit. As a child were you told that you have to work really hard to get what you need or desire? Did you get the message that working hard was the only way to succeed in life? Did you witness your parents constantly striving and stressed out? Was one of your parents a workaholic? These types of messages, both verbal and non-verbal, were internalized by you as truth. Do you think you don't deserve to relax and just enjoy life?

Hummingbirds eat nectar or sugar. Sugar represents joy and fun to me. The sugar rush we experience and the delicious taste may help you to understand why I personally see this symbolism. Hummingbird wants you to experience Joy! Savor the sweetness of life. Look for joy in the daily events of life as well as the special occasions. Being in joy is the best way to spread joy. Like a hummingbird you can "flit" from person to person pollinating the world with joy.

I'm also excited when I see a hummingbird. Their presence makes me feel happy. To me, this reinforces the message of joy and happiness.

What are your beliefs about joy and play? Do you remember as a child being chastised when you were playing for being too rambunctious? Were you allowed to play with abandon or were you put into structured play programs like sports, art classes, and other controlled, scheduled, manipulated events? If so, the belief may have formed that play for the sake of play is a waste of time. Not everything needs a purpose or goal attached to it. Playing is one of the most important aspects of childhood growth and development and sorely missing in our society. It's never too late to splash around in a mud puddle.

When I was about five years old my mother, brother, and I were at the grocery store. While my mother pushed the shopping cart and my brother walked along beside her, I was twisting across the store, keeping my feet together and shifting them diagonally to move from one tile square to the next. I had made up a little game for myself while listening to the background music.

"Mom," my brother said, "Tell Karen to stop dancing."

"I'm not dancing."

"Yes, she is," he said, "Tell her to stop."

"Karen, stop dancing." Mom said.

I stopped. At that precise moment I was programmed to believe that acting a certain way in public is more important than having fun.

If we unconsciously believe that play is a waste of time, pure play, joyful, uninhibited play, we lose part of what should be our most important occupation, experiencing joy. Hummingbirds remind us that play is a priority.

Was it a ruby throated hummingbird that you saw, with its beautiful, vibrant, iridescent colors? This is another message to go for it all. Enjoy the full spectrum of delights that life has to offer.

Did your religion emphasize seriousness and service above personal happiness? Children love to run, yell, and laugh. These are all aspects of joy. Were you told to sit still and keep quiet as a child? My grandmother once took me with her while she visited a friend. I was told to sit in a chair against the wall. It was a hard little kid-sized wooden chair. After a while I started to fidget. I wasn't really bored, I had an active mind; I was just moving a little. My grandmother told me in no uncertain terms to sit still. Her friend said, "Oh, she's just a child." But Nana was not having any of that. I know that her admonition had nothing to do with me. It was my grandmother's learned belief that children should be seen and not heard. She was just following her indoctrination. For me it was another lesson that acting in a socially prescribed way is more important than fun. It's called being appropriate. Forget appropriate. Be joyful, have fun, listen to Hummingbird's message.

The other part of rushing around and never stopping is avoidance. Do you keep yourself constantly busy to avoid your thoughts and emotions? Are there painful issues you need to deal with and rather than face them you keep yourself constantly in motion.

After using the information I already knew about hummingbirds, I decided to go a step further and do some investigating. I found that a hummingbird's heart rate is about 1200 beats per minute when flying and about 250 when resting. The first thing that popped into my mind is the idea of overworking, overdoing, and stressing out. What does that rapid heart rate make you think of? What does the heart represent to you?

The other bit of information I found interesting is that a hummingbird goes into a state of hibernation every night called torpor. Its heart slows to about 50 beats per minute and they may appear as if they aren't even breathing. Their body temperature drops. This made me think of meditation as our body slows down when we meditate. If a hummingbird didn't go into torpor it would die. The demands of its high metabolism would soon find it unable to feed itself enough to stay alive. As a metaphor relating to humans it might mean that without taking time to nurture ourselves with stillness and relaxation the stress in our lives would be overwhelming.

If we take time to quiet ourselves and go into stillness, we fare much better. Meditation is shown to lower blood pressure and heart rate. Cortisol (the stress hormone) levels drop, anxiety levels drop, inflammation responses are reduced, our self-esteem increases, memory loss is lessened, and a host of other physical and emotional benefits are delivered. We don't have to go into torpor to receive these amazing physical and emotional perks, meditation or still alertness of our environment will do.

Have you ever seen a hummingbird nest? I hadn't until I did the research. They are works of art. The hummingbird makes her tiny nest from small bits of soft, organic material. It uses its needle-like beak to intertwine spider web silk with the nesting materials and spreads the silk over the outside creating a fine velvety surface.

When it's done it's a lovely nest for the two tiny eggs she will lay.

Hummingbird wants us to make our homes nurturing places, lovely nests. She brings tidings of comfort and joy. Our home can be small and modest as well as a soft, safe sanctuary for us.

Her two eggs represent balance. We need to work and play, to move and to rest, to create and to admire. Hummingbird's biggest message is to enjoy life, every aspect of it, the work and the play. If you see a hummingbird, enjoy the experience, and bring that joy into your life.

What is your favorite animal? What animal excites you when you see it? What traits in those animals do you admire or label as negative? Do you share any of the traits? What is special to you about them?

CHAPTER 6

Burning up the Lines

Back in the days of wall phones Janice was in her kitchen cooking dinner for Ted, a man she'd been seeing. While she was cooking the phone rang. It was on the wall next to the stove. She picked it up and it was Ted calling to let her know that he wouldn't be able to make it for dinner. He had cancelled several times in the previous weeks. He was supposed to be there in an hour.

Janice's reaction was to tell him that it was no problem, don't worry about it, everything's wonderful. Suddenly the line went dead. Janice was stirring a pot while she talked on the phone and the flame on the gas stove had burned through the phone cord.

Do you think Janice really had no problem with Ted calling at the last minute to cancel after she had gone to the trouble to cook him dinner? What does a phone represent? What does it do? It allows us to communicate. On an emotional level the phone would represent expressing our selves. Janice was communicating with her mouth that she didn't mind him cancelling once again. She wasn't connected on a conscious level to her emotions, her anger. But, on an unconscious level she was very connected to her anger. Fire symbolism shows us just how angry she was. It burned her up! She was fuming (gas stove)! She wanted to see him burn! She was ready to explode! She was seeing red! She was at the boiling point (pot on stove)! This was an easy interpretation. The negative symbolism of fire is anger. Burning through your phone cord is certainly a good indication that we should be looking at the negative interpretation of fire. If Janice can see the fire symbolism as an indication of how deeply buried her anger is, she can make some progress in dealing with repressed emotions.

Janice needs to learn to express anger in a healthy way and not suppress her feeling. If she keeps suppressing her anger she will explode, maybe through an aneurism or a heart attack. Blocked emotions may cause blockages in our bodies. The positive symbolism of fire is passion, creativity. Perhaps if we find creative outlets and enjoy creative pursuits on a regular basis it may help us release some of that anger and resentment in a healthier way.

If you tend to get burned, while cooking, or doing whatever, look at how you deal with your anger. If you have a fire in your oven or wherever, question it. Are you afraid to show anger? Were you taught that children don't get angry, only smiles allowed here? As a child did you witness terrible outbursts of anger that scared you? You may have developed a belief that anger was dangerous and that you would not be safe or you would lose control if you expressed anger. Take a good look at the childhood lessons you learned about expressing yourself. Are they healthy lessons or would you do well to re-evaluate your approach to your emotions and how you react? Can you think of other ways you were subconsciously taught to deal with your emotions?

Did you ever see either of your parents cry? How did they express their emotions in front of you? Were they honest and open about feelings or did they try to pretend that everything was wonderful all the time in front of their children? Did they express emotions in unhealthy ways that upset or frightened you? What traits have you picked up? How were you taught to deal with anger through the lens of your childhood eyes? Do you want to respond in the same way your authority figures did?

Anger Dream: I was in a parking lot walking towards a store when I saw a police officer screaming at someone. I went over and told him that there was no need to act that way. I told him that he could be angry and let someone know what was wrong without screaming at them and being a bully.

What does this dream mean? The policeman represented the part of me that was having a hard time dealing with anger issues in a healthy way. I was certainly policing my anger; it never got out. My father tended to have angry outbursts that frightened me. Perhaps I was afraid that I would completely lose control if I started to express my anger. The message of the dream is what I told the policeman. You can effectively deal with your anger without hurting others or yourself.

Janice needed to learn how to express her anger and figure out why she felt she should put up with behavior that left her feeling unappreciated and taken for granted. Looking at her childhood and the way her parents and authority figures handled their emotional responses will give her great insight. Reviewing how she was cherished or not as a child will tell her why she accepts a partner that doesn't value her. You are valuable, you are worthy and loved.

CHAPTER 7

Down the Rabbit Hole

Recently I found a dead rabbit under my back deck. I was in the kitchen doing some mundane chores when I heard cats fighting outside. Running out the back door I saw my cat, and another come flying out from under the deck. They disappeared into the brush at the property line.

Two days later I set out to water my garden and had to go under the deck to turn on the hose. That's when I found the dead rabbit. Something about finding a dead animal at my house screams symbolic message to me. The more we know about an animal the easier it will be to interpret the symbolism. If you don't have the means at the time to research an animal just think of what you do know and focus on the first thoughts that come to mind. Old sayings and idioms suggest symbolic meaning as well. You've heard the expression, "multiply like rabbits." This is positive symbolism to me, implying abundance. Also ask how the animal makes you feel? Do you think they are cute, sweet, clever, dangerous, power-ful, or aggressive?

When I see a rabbit in its natural habitat, like in a field eating clover, it's usually on high alert. Its nose is constantly twitching, asking if any predators are nearby. Its eyes dart about, its ears are attuned to the slightest sound. It is ready to run in an instant. They stay close to the ground and are always aware of the nearest hiding place. They're furry balls of nervous, anxious energy. I chose the negative traits of the rabbit in this instance because it was dead, certainly not a positive trait for a rabbit. I would say in the negative symbolism they represent fear and anxiety. What are your negative perceptions of rabbits?

Our backyard represents our past; it's easy to see how that makes sense, it is behind us. The rabbit was under my deck, behind my house. Fear was a big part of my past and there's still some work to do on releasing fear and anxiety from my life. Fear and anxiety are still present in the dark subconscious under my deck.

What kind of childhood conditioning may cause us to be fearful and anxious as adults? Were our parents overly protective? Did they live life to the fullest or were their lives, like most people, predicated on the roles they were taught? Did our parents instill in us a sense of adventure, or did they pursue security and conformity? Were they always expecting the worst outcome or a fairy tale ending? Having a parent that is inconsistent in their behavior and emotions can cause us to be anxious and fearful because we never know what to expect and so we are constantly walking on eggshells, fearing the worst, always in fight or flight mode.

To me, death symbolizes change; it is a transition from one state of being to another. Some say to a better state. The death symbolism here suggests that I am afraid (rabbit) of change. I don't want to leave my comfortable familiar life (the past) for the unknown, though the unknown may bring me to a better place.

The cat killed the rabbit, so it features prominently in the interpretation. The cat lives in my house, in the present. What does a cat symbolize? We'll look at its traits to decipher the meaning. I think a cat does what it wants, when it wants, and how it wants. It doesn't allow anyone that it doesn't want to enter its personal space. It asks for affection when it wants it and will walk away when it wants to be left alone. A cat sets clear and healthy boundaries. A cat is content with its own company. It doesn't let anyone influence its behavior. A cat is autonomous. When thinking of what an animal symbolizes, what it means to you is the most important part of your interpretation. To me the positive symbolism of a cat is healthy boundaries, and the negative is selfishness and a disrespect of others' boundaries. Your thoughts on the symbolism of a cat might vary significantly from mine.

In my interpretation, the questions raised would be about setting personal boundaries. How was I taught as a child, and reinforced as an adult, that I had to do what I didn't want and that it was okay to invade my personal space both physically and emotionally? Let me count the ways.

Children are often forced to hug or kiss someone even though they don't want to. A grandfather may tell a child that if they give him a hug, they'll get a reward of some sort. This puts the child in a situation of having to give up control of their bodies to get what they want. In essence they are taught to sell themselves. When someone tickles a child until they are crying and defends their actions by saying they are just playing they are overstepping a child's boundaries. We need to let children know their bodies are their own, they can say No to anything that doesn't feel right. In this way we also help them to trust their intuition and respect their right to autonomy. Teaching children it's all right to follow their gut and say no is empowering to them and increases their physical safety.

Our parents overstepped boundaries every time they tried to silence our authentic self. They wanted us to fit in believing it would bring us happiness. They wanted us to grow up and have a stable job believing that would bring us security. They were trying to protect us but were limiting our potential, just as their parents limited them with the prevailing cultural paradigms.

The rabbit under the deck represented the fear that ruled me in the past and still does or I wouldn't have received this symbolism. I used to live a life based entirely in fear, a life without taking risks, a life of self-doubt, anxiety, and constant vigil. I stayed in jobs I hated, in bad relationships, and saw myself as a victim of circumstance. The message is to realize that just because something happened in the past it doesn't predict the future. We can decide to stop living in fear.

The cat represents the part of me that does what it wants and claims its own authority by "killing" the fear driven life. It tells me I am the creator of my life and to kill any fear keeping me from moving forward with my dreams.

If, like the cat, we do what we want to do, we will be living our authentic, fulfilled life, unaffected by our past. Set healthy boundaries with people and circumstances in your life. Ask questions about how much you are willing to suffer for a sense of security. Do you believe you need to sacrifice your happiness to be financially stable? This is an almost universal paradigm. Are you afraid to do what you truly love?

Do most of us live ordinary lives, follow patterns, assume roles? Of course. We have been conditioned since the day we were born to assume a specific role and follow a prescribed lifestyle. Until we are aware we are not aware we are at the mercy of our conditioning and will suffer the consequences. Once aware we begin making conscious decisions about our life. Conscious living is paramount to fulfilling our purpose.

It may help to write down the experiences you believe have symbolic meaning. In this account I wrote I was doing "mundane" chores in the kitchen when I heard the cats screeching. This tells me that my "cat self" was calling me to kill my "rabbit self" or my life would be a series of "mundane" tasks, a life of tedium. If I hadn't written this, I may not have seen the symbolism of the first sentence. You don't have to take the step of writing, especially if it will hinder you in the search for symbolic messages in your life. Do what makes you happy and don't feel guilty about it. Be a cat.

When I went back under the deck to remove the rabbit, I saw there was a total of three dead rabbits there. I left a dead rabbit under my deck for two days and it multiplied. This increase in dead rabbits, representing fear and anxiety, tells me the message is intensified or magnified. To me it means fear will only bring more fear. Anxiety breeds anxiety. Fearful thoughts attract more fearful thoughts. Worry often brings with it the tape loop of imagined conversations and visions of doom. When someone has an anxiety attack it starts slowly and escalates. When we start to worry it escalates. When we go into fear it escalates. When you find a dead rabbit under your deck and don't do anything, the symbolism escalates until you heed its message.

The next time you find yourself worrying turn the dialogue around. Many of you have heard this metaphor before; if you are tuned into radio station WFEAR you are going to get their programming; if you change the station and tune into WJOY you are going to get their programming. It's a frequency match.

Start imagining the life you want to lead. Think about all the wonderful things that could happen. See yourself succeeding. Imagine people congratulating you. Thinking about what could go right, the future you want, is exciting and inspiring.

When we become aware that we are on a negative thought track the first thing we can do is acknowledge it. "My thoughts are negative right now. I am thinking things will go wrong, I will fail, nobody loves me, I am not good enough." Then we can recognize the thoughts for what they are, lies and negative projections. These thoughts come from experiences that conditioned us to believe we are not enough. These thoughts aren't helpful and don't predict our future. We are not our conditioned thoughts, we are more. When you interrupt your negative, conditioned mindset take a moment to congratulate yourself for recognizing the pattern. When you are in this frequency it is time to change your vibration. To lift yourself, think of a happy memory, tell yourself a joke, look at something beautiful, take a walk in nature, read an inspirational book or positive daily reminder, anything that will take you out of that vibration. This is the first step in mindfulness. You are not your thoughts. You are a Divine Being of Unlimited Potential!

Rituals are often used to symbolize a Rite of Passage, a new level of growth. It is a symbolic way of sealing a commitment to a new way of life. I used the ritual of burial to reinforce my intention to move forward without fear. I took a shovel and dug a hole. I used the shovel to lift the rabbits and place them in the hole and bury them. I laid my fears to rest. I buried the past.

Since I first wrote this story of my cat and the dead rabbits, I have had yet another experience involving my cat and a rabbit. The synchronicities keep on coming. I was walking my dog in the park; my cat often accompanies us. I heard my cat at my feet and looked down to see it had brought me a gift, a very small baby rabbit. The baby rabbit was still quite alive, and the cat was playing with it. I scooped the cat up into my arms. Then I saw my dog was trying to get the rabbit. I pulled my dog away from the rabbit so it might escape. I quickly brought my dog and cat home.

I went back to the park to check and found the baby rabbit had run off. What does this mean? Since this bunny got away it is a positive symbol. Rabbits in their positive aspects represent abundance. Nothing multiplies more than rabbits. This experience tells me that when I stop living in fear, I will experience increased abundance. Since it was a baby rabbit, the idea of abundance was magnified as the baby (like a seed) will grow, become bigger, and multiply. I saw it as a message that I was successfully cementing my belief that I deserve abundance and have nothing to fear. My cat, representing the part of me living an authentic life, brought me the gift of abundance.

Don't do what you dread and hate. Do what brings you happiness and your ideal abundant life will emerge. I prefer an abundance of joy to any other form of abundance, but I'll accept them all.

CHAPTER 8

The Open I

Before we start this chapter make sure you are comfortably seated and relaxed. Close your eyes and think of a body part, any body part, the first body part that jumps into your mind. Don't try to figure out which body part is correct. There is no wrong answer. After you've thought of a particular body part open your eyes and read on.

A very talented Polarity therapist once asked me to close my eyes and think of a body part. After a few seconds I replied that all I could see was a closed eye.

She tilted her head and looked at me waiting for me to get it. Sadly, it took me a few moments before I grasped that the eye was I. I was the closed I. It was true, at that point in my life I was pretty shut down. I was closed off from emotions, from self-awareness, from relationships, and from my spiritual self.

I was also closed off from my feminine side. When I walked into her studio, I noticed that she looked so feminine in her flowy skirt and blouse. I was wearing jeans and a shirt in a very masculine design. I could have been a lumberjack. After I was there for a few minutes she brought it up, suggesting, in a kind and compassionate way, that I was suppressing my feminine side. The feminine side of us is open and receptive. It is nurturing and creative. This reinforced my vision of the closed I. I was not open and receptive. Suppressing my feminine open side closed me to potential and possibility. I was conditioned in my childhood to believe that female was inferior. I was not honoring my feminine nature, the magnificence and power that is the Divine Feminine. I was not nurturing myself.

Due to my unconscious belief that masculine was more important and mattered more (instilled by my father from his cultural indoctrination) I carried shame about my feminine gender. I saw it as inferior. I believed I was invisible, unimportant, held no value. It took a long time for me to recognize the magnificence of the Divine Feminine energy. I now embrace the Divine Feminine. In a world that is off balance it is important for everyone, men and women, to embrace the Feminine Energy of the Divine Mother.

What part of your body came to mind? What does it represent? Consider the symbolism of that part of the body. Is it your throat? That may represent communication or expression. Are you truthful and open in your communication, are you direct, or do you stifle responses for fear of being embarrassed or overstepping? Do you speak in a kind and loving manner? The Bahai faith wants us to consider these four questions before we speak: Is it Kind? Is it necessary? Is it true? Does it improve on the silence? If we can answer in the affirmative to these questions then we should speak up, if not it's better to remain silent. The throat representing expression also refers to how you express yourself vibrationally. Are you expressing love or fear?

Is it your legs? That may represent moving forward in life. Are you feeling stagnant, like you're not moving forward? Is it your breasts? That may represent nurturing. Is it your elbows? That may represent how you enfold and embrace life. What does the function of the body part you saw make you think of? What are some idioms used for that body part? Are you taking a bite out of life or allowing life to chew you up and spit you out? Do you have a finger in every little detail of your life and everyone else's? Are you shouldering too much responsibility? Are you sitting on your butt or going after what you want?

This exercise told me a lot about myself. I now celebrate my feminine nature and am proud to be in this club of amazing people, men included, who recognize the importance of the Divine Feminine and claim it for themselves. If nothing immediately comes to mind concerning the body part that you thought of, just ask yourself what it means and wait for the answer. I believe it will be enlightening for you as well.

CHAPTER 9

Forgive and Follow Your Intuition

At an Abundance Class I recently attended the topic of forgiveness was being addressed. I've been working on forgiveness for years. The Abundance course wanted us to list our resentments from the past and how they made us feel, as well as our personal part in creating the situations.

I have done so much work on forgiveness and life reviews that I felt doing this wouldn't serve me and in fact didn't want to revisit the negative stories of my life. It's a wonderful exercise, but when you're done with it you don't need to review the same stories over and over.

If something still pushes our buttons, we do need to revisit it and put it to rest. I was feeling like I would rather have any issues that I might still have return to me organically when I was ready for another round of forgiveness and understanding. When I'm ready the triggers will come. I wanted to follow my personal Divine Order and not the syllabus of the class. Due to my indoctrination

that I must follow the rules set up in the class I was resist-
ing my preference to skip the exercise.

Forgiveness is an important part of giving up our
conditioning and moving to consciousness. We need
to bring our shadow selves into the light, forgive all past
hurts, and release blame and anger. If we continue to tell
the same sad story we may want to question if we really
have let the emotions attached to that story go. What
are we getting out of being in the victim role by telling
others our sad story? What is the reward; is it attention,
sympathy, a feeling of superiority over the people who
have hurt us? We may not believe it is affecting our
lives, but if we are attached to the telling of a story then
it still holds some power over us. A good indicator is if
you can tell the story and laugh. If telling the story still
causes even the smallest catch in your throat or hesita-
tion in your speech it is still having an effect on you. It
may help to think of the antagonist in your story as a
child. How were they hurt and abused? Remind yourself
that wounded people wound others. You are not hurt by
these people because of some defect in yourself but because of a deep hurt that still resides in the heart of the
person assaulting you. They would have done better if
they could. Then decide if you are going to do better and
forgive them, or if you are going to continue the cycle
and become bitter. If you haven't heard these expressions before then listen up ~ If you don't become better,
you become bitter ~ Blame is a game you will never win.
I may have made the second one up.

A parent or caregiver might have sincerely believed
that the best thing for you was corporal punishment, or
persuading you to become a doctor, sending you to diet

camp or boarding school. Their decisions on how to guide you were based on the erroneous beliefs with which they were raised. They weren't acting from a place of knowing their own Divinity and seeing your Divinity. They were acting from a place of ego pain or indoctrination. Unless someone is acting from Source Consciousness, which is true Love, they are acting from fear.

But they beat me, you may say. They locked me in my room. They were drunk all the time and I went hungry. They didn't even try. They told me they wished I had never been born. They didn't love me. It is hard to believe that someone is doing the best they can when you see others doing so much better. The most wounded egos attack and escape. It is all they know, and it is a terrible learned behavior. If they had been given what they needed, they would have done better. They are incapable until they begin to awaken, to ask questions about their lives and to understand that they are conditioned. We can be the ones to break the cycle.

I'm sure you know many people who have never changed. Change is frightening to the ego. The ego fears dying. If we start to change, if we see a better way without the ego, we may no longer require the ego's false message of fear. The ego will do almost anything to keep you from waking up to your True Self. It will even remind you of all the people you can blame for your current situation. It will tell you that others are the problem and if only they would change then your life would improve. We can only change ourselves. We can't change our past and we certainly can't change another person. Dr. Einstein was right, "You can't change the situation you're in with the same consciousness that created it."

Look at workplace situations when new management arrives and immediately wants to change everything. Everyone panics, complains, and thinks about quitting. A few may recognize that there is always upheaval with change, and they will try to counsel their peers to calm down and let the process emerge. These people are more likely to grow in their personal lives because they know that change is difficult, but it's not going to kill them. They know they'll get through it and that the outcome may be better than where they started. Workplace change is not a personal attack.

In fact, nothing is ever personal. When someone treats you badly, it is always from a belief in their own unworthiness. It is about their misconceptions, lack of trust, and fear. Accept that their wounds precipitated the attack. Attack is a strong word, but anything that isn't Love is an attack. It comes from a place of defensiveness. Something in our behavior triggered a feeling in them that they were being threatened. You aren't responsible for their perceptions or reactions. Most negative reactions are trigger responses.

It's hard to believe that a child can be threatening to a parent, but a child pushes many of the parent's wounded childhood buttons just by its being. A parent may behave very differently to the child who holds the same birth order as them or is the same gender. They often over-identify with one of their children. They may feel especially protective of the child with whom they identify, or they may have higher expectations of that child. Conversely, they may feel especially resentful of a child who is in the same birth order or of the same gender as one of their siblings who made their life miserable or whom their parents favored. They are projecting. Parents often react to their children from their own familial history.

I had an old childhood friend who had her own family, a boy, then a girl. The same order of gender as her birth family. Growing up, my friend's older brother had been very cruel to her. I ran into her on the sidewalk one day as she was pushing the stroller with her young daughter in it and her three-year old son walking beside it. While we were talking the three-year-old reached into the stroller, not at all in an aggressive manner, just to touch his sister. My friend grabbed his arm and hissed at him, "Don't you touch your sister!"

It was quite alarming to me, and I can't imagine what went through her son's mind. To me it seemed obvious that she was reacting in complete identification with her daughter. Her daughter represented her, and her three-year-old son represented her older brother. She was living in the past and letting her wounded child raise her children. If she had been able to see the source of her anger, recognize that she was replaying a pattern, and, if she could, ideally forgive her brother, she may have been able to raise her children without the influence of her unhealed childhood wounds.

If your parents are still on this plane you may be able to form a conscious, authentic relationship with them. Using the affirmation, "My parents and I hold each other in love and respect," may help. Repeat it throughout the day. You don't need to tell them about it or have them participate. Your intention will change how you see them. This works with any family and friends, "My children and I hold each other in love and respect."

Having worked so much on forgiveness my intuition told me that any residual anger and resentment I might foster would surface at the right time and place. I wanted to trust in Divine Order. But I felt guilty for not following the abundance class syllabus. I was waffling about what to do.

The day after the assignment was given, I was driving my sister to the airport in her car. She had asked me to pick up some flooring for her at a store not too far out of my way on the ride home. She told me she had the GPS system set to the store's address and to turn it on after I dropped her off.

Something went terribly wrong. Coming out of Logan International in Boston it guided me through the Ted Williams tunnel and then back the other way, then it sent me to Downtown Crossing, and all over Boston. It was nerve wracking. Finally, I decided to just go the way I had planned and immediately felt better. I told myself to go to the Tobin Bridge. I turned a corner and there was a sign for the Tobin Bridge. I completely relaxed and headed to Route 95. When I exited 95 and was on the street where the store was located I put the GPS back on but it cut out and wasn't working. I decided to find the store the old-fashioned way and again felt better. I immediately pulled into a parking lot to check the street numbers and found myself directly in front of the store.

If this isn't a message to follow my intuition and not the guidance of someone else or my ego, I don't know what is. I was literally following a guidance system that was not my own and getting lost. Since I was driving my sister's car, I would also look at what the first thing was that came to mind when I thought of my sister in relation to following intuition. The answer reflects the part of me that is having trouble following my own inner voice. The moment I decided to follow my own inner guidance I started going in the right direction, in fact ending up exactly where I was supposed to be. Our guidance system is our Intuition. Do what feels right in your heart.

Can you think of times when you second guessed yourself and things went wrong? Did you receive signs that you were on the wrong track? Were you rewarded when you chose to follow your inner guidance? If we find ourselves taking the wrong exits on the highway it may be a sign that we aren't following our intuition in some area of our lives. Remember roads represent our path in life. Are you frequently finding that you are lost, whether hiking in the woods or on a road trip? Where are you veering off the path of personal growth and happiness? Do you trust your intuition? It is Divine Guidance from your own Higher Self.

Who do you want to forgive? Do you know anything about their journey and their beliefs about themselves? Can you imagine that an attack isn't personal, but a feeling of fear in the other person? Can you see them as someone in pain? Can you see them as a wounded child? That is often the first step in forgiving. We expect less from children, as we should, and when someone is expressing from childhood wounds it is as if we are dealing with a child. We don't have to stick around to be abused by someone, but we can forgive and remove ourselves from attack.

CHAPTER 10

I Can See Clearly Now

Trisha was attending an intensive month-long Yoga teacher training at a large ashram. She had chosen this course because of its emphasis on the spiritual aspects of Yoga. A lot of people believe Yoga is purely a physical practice, but the true goal of Yoga is enlightenment. Hatha Yoga, the asanas or poses, is used to prepare the body for meditation and enlightenment. It's hard to sit in meditation in an uncomfortable body.

One of the Swamis teaching and mentoring the students was a retired Marine. He had been in the military service for over twenty years. It seemed a strange place for a Marine to end up, a place of peace and love. He was a man of such grace that the students often sought him out for counsel and words of wisdom.

One day while taking a break in the center green, Trish and a few other students were sitting on the lawn talking with the Swami about dreams and symbols. Trish told him about her dream from the previous night. In it she was living in a tall wooden tower in a forest. She climbed the many flights of stairs to the very top room. In front of her were three windows that looked out at the crowns of tall pine trees. As she gazed out at the beautiful pines the middle window suddenly popped out and tumbled to the ground far below leaving her with a clear view of the green forest.

The Swami told her that the dream meant that her third eye was very close to opening. She was right at the "breaking point" of awakening to her Divinity. The third eye is located between and slightly above our physical eyes. It is the "eye of God." It allows us to "see" Truth, to clearly see Heavenly Love. Trish had been practicing meditation for a long time and this interpretation pleased her.

The tower would represent her frequency rising. The stairs of the tower represent the Chi, Divine Energy, rising through her center, her spine. Each level would represent a higher Chakra. This is sometimes referred to as Jacob's Ladder.

The highest tower room and the tops of the pine trees represent the Crown Chakra (at the crown of our head) where Spiritual Energy enters our body. We've all heard the expression that the eyes are the windows to the soul. In the dream the window "opened." It popped right out. Her third eye "opened." There is nothing clearer than a window without glass. There is no distortion, we see only Truth.

In the physical world, windows represent our eyes. They are what we look through to see the world outside of our home (body). Imagine that the windows in your home are dirty. It's hard to see past the dirt that is clouding the windows. Symbolically, the dirt is our indoctrination, our unconscious beliefs, and is distorting our view of who we truly are. The dirt on the windows represents the lies that we were told. If we can clean these windows, release the lies, we would see that we are nothing less than a Divine Creation of God. We are not the roles prescribed to us. We are not the worthless child that we were taught we are. We are not unimportant. We are not ugly, we are not failures, we are not less than anyone else. You are perfect as you are. You are magnificent as you are. Wipe away the dirt and see your true limitless self. See the Truth.

Clean the windows in your home as a symbol of your new vision of yourself. As you clean them look through the clear glass and know that you are seeing the world and yourself anew. You are seeing a Divine Manifestation of God born to express the love of the Christ to all. You are exactly who you are supposed to be. See yourself as the unique and necessary shining example of God's creation that you are. Everyone you see through the windows, through your eyes, are also magnificent creations of the One Consciousness.

CHAPTER 11

Cheerleaders in the Basement

Dream: I opened the basement door and looked down the stairs. It was an enormous deep basement, two stories high, well lit, and spacious. In the middle of the large space a cheerleading squad was practicing, led by their coach. They were in full cheerleader regalia, jumping and cheering. Though unfinished, the basement had smooth, clean cement floors and walls. I walked down the long two-story flight of stairs. Against the far wall was a very small room, just the size of a closet. I opened the door and there was a toilet. I went in, closed the door behind me, and sat down on the toilet to do my business. As I sat on the toilet, I could hear the cheerleaders finishing up their practice, packing their gym bags, and getting ready to leave. I heard them climbing the stairs. I got a little nervous and reached over to open the door a crack. I peeked out to see the last cheerleader was about to switch off the lights. I yelled, "Don't turn out the lights, I'm still down here." End of dream.

Let's deconstruct this dream to see what it means. It takes place in the basement, which is below ground level, so it represents my subconscious. The basement is empty which would signify I've pretty much cleared out my programmed subconscious beliefs. I've done a lot of work on my belief system, how I acquired it, and what parts of it I want to discard. I have cleaned out my basement.

Since everyone in our dreams represents a different aspect of our self it appears I've been cheering myself on, being my own life coach, using affirmations, enthusiasm, and inspiration to lift myself above the limiting belief systems I was taught. I've realized the lies I was raised to believe are *false identities and limiting constructs produced by a collective social agreement based in fear.*

The cheerleader aspect of me has been encouraging and supporting me, "You can do it! You're not less than anyone because your father said so, not because you danced in public, not because you're a girl, not because of your age or height or intellect. You are the perfect incarnation of Love." The cheerleader reaching in to turn out the light is the part of me telling me my cheerleading job is done. We can only go so far with positive self-talk, affirmations, and enthusiasm. It takes some soul work, not just cheerleading to realize who we truly are. We must understand the hurts we've experienced, the pain that we perceive was caused by others, have absolutely no bearing on who we are. I work to be mindful of my thoughts. I ask for discernment. I ask my Higher Self to take charge of my ego self. I spend time in stillness through meditation every day. The small self, the ego can only go so far in helping us awaken, we need the Higher Self to make us new.

I yelled from my perch on the toilet to the cheerleader to keep the light on. This is because I still needed the light to shine on the remaining subconscious issues from my childhood interfering with my growth. I can't allow the light to be turned off until I have uncovered all the beliefs that led me to fear and feelings of unworthiness. I must recognize every conditioned construct that hinders my joy and purpose in this life.

I'm on the toilet when I yell to the cheerleader to keep the light on. What do you think that means? It means I still have some sh*t to deal with. Some symbolism is that obvious. The Universe clearly has a sense of humor.

I can enhance and expand this dream's symbolism by closing my eyes and visualizing taking a flashlight and exploring the basement, shining a light on any fears and false beliefs that may still be lurking in a dark corner, waiting for the perfect moment to instill fear and bring me back down to ego thinking. If you close your eyes and imagine a similar scene you may be surprised at what you see when you shine light in these dark places.

In the dream the basement is unfinished. As another exercise I can imagine finishing the basement with inspiring images of love, joy, and abundance. By seeing this basement beautifully finished I am claiming there is no room for lies and beliefs that inhibit me. Now it is filled with my worthiness. I can imagine this basement as a beautiful garden filled with blossoming flowers. I can see it excavated and fully above ground with windows all around bringing in golden Divine Light. A place that shines with pure unconditional love.

You can use symbolism to help you identify your own erroneous fears. Go down into your imaginary basement and shine the light. What do you see? An animal? A relic from your past? A person you know? How do you respond? Can you imagine yourself holding your hands up to any negative imagery and magically turning it into pure golden light? Fill it with Love. Be gentle with yourself and remember to be your own cheerleader.

CHAPTER 12

Creepy Crawlies

Let's look at probably the most common fear of the external, that of spiders. The reason this fear is so common is that it symbolizes a fear that many people have, the fear of being themselves, of completely expressing who they are. We all try to suppress our true selves, our true feelings opting instead to be "normal," to fit in, and be loved. This fear is compounded by the messages in the media of how we are supposed to look and act. Oh my, what will people think if I do what I want to do? To be authentic is to be your unique self and that's scary. Why does a spider represent authenticity?

Most web spinning spiders have very poor eyesight. A vibration in their web lets them know if they have caught a scrumptious bug. A male spider does a special mating dance on a female's web to let her know he is there, ready to mate with her. A spider depends on vibration for information and to make decisions.

Vibration symbolizes our intuition, our energy, our frequency. It is our Divine Self sending us messages. The science of physics tells us all is energy. How can we make a decision for our highest good if it comes only from our five senses? How we physically perceive is incredibly limited by our senses and subjective at best as it is strongly influenced by our indoctrination. Energy is everything and therefore has all answers.

For hundreds of years the scientific world was based on the paradigm of Newtonian Mechanics. We are now in the Age of Quantum Mechanics, yet this new and vital knowledge has not informed our science or medicine. It's time to utilize the realization that energy is the basis of human life and we can change and heal ourselves by raising our vibration, our frequency, our connection to the Source Energy we are. I predict energy healing and frequency healing will become more accepted as people open to the science of Quantum Mechanics.

Our Divine Self doesn't vibrate at the frequency of matter; it vibrates at the frequency of Love. What we see before us in the physical world are the collective and personal creations of ego, of the small self. Ego decisions are based in fear, the fear we are taught as children. Our best decisions come from our Higher Self. Spiders tell us to trust our Intuition above all other senses to inform us.

Why are spiders such a big symbol of fear? Because we are all afraid that if we open to the highest vibration of Source we will lose ourselves. We are afraid our personality will disappear. We are afraid due to our conditioning that we are unworthy of Divine Love. All we give up, to be our true self, is our fear, our constant anxious thoughts, and our self-destructive patterns. These patterns are so familiar to us that we are afraid of losing them because we believe we are the patterns. We falsely believe they protect us when they actually preclude us from any progress.

Female spiders are much larger than their male counterparts. This tells us spiders represent the Divine Feminine. We are talking about energy here, not gender. We all have some feminine (yin, open, intuitive, receptive, nurturing) energy and some masculine (yang, action, movement, productive, get things done) energy.

As the Feminine, the spiders represent intuition, nurturing, creativity, and abundance. The Divine Feminine is about openness. The spider reminds us that just as they shoot silk out to create their web, we shoot thoughts and beliefs out into the universe and create our lives. Spiders' silk is sent out in a straight line. This symbolism tells us to focus on a goal after we have made a decision based in our intuition. Are our thoughts focused on a goal or do we have scattered thoughts and beliefs that cannot produce results?

If we don't believe we are worthy and deserving of an amazing and abundant life than the universe can't provide it for us. The Universe follows our focus and direction. If on some unconscious level we still believe those voices that tell us we aren't important then our vibration transmits that energy and it is reflected back to us as our life. Everything in our life is created by our beliefs, which create our thoughts, which determine our emotions and our actions. Once we get into a loop of negativity the emotions, thoughts, and beliefs feed each other.

Through stopping our continuous thought process, even for a few moments, we begin our journey into consciousness and peace. We can distract ourselves with happy memories. Meditation is another way to stop a negative track. Being in the present moment always stops our thoughts. Seeing something of beauty, like a sunset, stops our thoughts. These things are temporary, but with each moment of stillness we create a step on our path. The more we are present the more steps we move forward.

Why does a spider spin a web? It uses it to catch food, to nurture itself. Is the life you are manifesting with your beliefs and thoughts nurturing you? Are your beliefs telling you that you are worthy? What web of thoughts are you spinning? Is it a web of lies? Do you believe you will never have abundance? Do you believe money is for other people? Know you are worthy. Know you deserve abundance as much as anyone else. Your beliefs about who you are will determine what you catch in your personal web. Do you believe you are lovable? Only you can determine your worth. Cast out a web that brings you happiness and abundance.

Spider's web is made through connecting strands of silk. Spider silk is one of the strongest natural materials on earth, stronger than steel and very elastic. At the same diameter steel will break before spider silk. Steel is rigid, spider silk is flexible. Your beliefs are as strong as spider's silk. Choose your beliefs wisely, don't accept what you were programmed to believe. You are flexible and can change. Beliefs are the determining factor in the life you manifest. Do you have strong bonds with others? Are you flexible with others, not letting your egoic standards, ethics, or personal moral code interfere with how you hold them in your heart? Are you flexible enough to be open to new ways of considering things, new possibilities in your life, or are you determined to continue exactly as you are, believing that your way is the best way? Don't believe everything you think.

To me the most interesting aspect of spider symbolism is the way a spider uses its blood to open itself. A spider has muscles to pull its legs in but doesn't have muscles to move its legs out. It uses a hydraulic system of pumping blood into its legs to open them. Blood represents joy. We want joy to flow through us, don't we! Legs signify moving forward, they are what carry us through life, bring us down the paths we choose, and help us progress in our journey. Spider is telling us to move forward in joy, expressing ourselves in joy by doing what we want.

A spider's blood is blue. Blue is the color of the fifth chakra, the throat chakra. Think of the symbolism of your throat. Remember, we determine symbolism by asking questions. What does your throat do? It allows you to eat. Eating is about feeding and nurturing yourself, so Spider is telling you to nurture your dreams, nurture your joy. Feed your soul with inspiring words and sights. Instead of watching the news, watch inspiring videos from people who have been on a path to joy. Read inspirational books to reinforce your joy. Don't put off the things you want to do. Is there something important to you that you want to accomplish? Do it! Take the dance class! Write the book! Visit that destination! Follow your dream! Commit to nurturing your soul.

Your throat is also your means of expression, but the symbolism goes beyond your physical voice. Spider says express yourself, not the role you were told to follow, but the life you choose. Self-expression, living your truth, is the way to Joy! Don't be a small self, following a path laid out for you by society, your parents, your indoctrination. When you move forward doing what you are called to do, trusting all you need for the journey will present itself to you, you will experience ongoing joy, contentment, and peace.

Expressing the Love you are, expressing the joy of Source Energy, is the most important form of expression.

Spiders molt. Molting symbolizes leaving what you have outgrown. We outgrow conditioned beliefs, we outgrow false identities, we outgrow relationships, we outgrow behaviors and habits. Leave it all behind. Don't be afraid to step into the larger you! The new and improved you. The You Who Knows the Truth of who you are.

We can't talk about spiders without talking about the number eight. A spider has eight legs, eight eyes, and its body is shaped like the number eight. Eight is the number of money and power, of abundance on the physical plane.

The number eight also represents balance, you can see this in the two circles that comprise the numeral eight. The symbol of eight is also the symbol of infinity; an eight person can have it all.

Look at all the different aspects of spider symbolism. As the spider says, "your intuition will tell you which symbols are meant for you." The biggest take away I get from spider is to choose a life that brings you joy.

CHAPTER 13

Buddha Frog

If you have a memory, some experience or situation that keeps coming into your consciousness, it may be there is a lesson in the experience for you now. At the time of the experience, you may not have been able to decipher its symbolic meaning, it's resurfacing now when it is once again relevant to your life, and you have the tools necessary to understand it.

Here is a memory of mine that has jumped into my consciousness recently. My family lived on a pond when I was growing up. My grandmother's house was next door, and she had a cat that would catch large fat bullfrogs and eat their hind legs. I would find these poor unfortunate frogs sitting in the grass unable to move. Placing a frog on a lily pad in the water at the edge of the pond I would pour water over its head to keep it cool and comfortable. The frog seemed content as I did this. It reminded me of a wise old man with its big belly and peaceful countenance. Eventually my mother would come out and take me into the house, explaining that keeping the frog alive was doing it a disservice and it would be better off if I allowed it to die. I was only six, but I understood what she was telling me.

What messages are there in these memories for me that I was unable to recognize as a small child?

Let's start with the frog facts. Frogs are amphibians, they live in the water, but do come on land occasionally. They lay gelatinous egg sacks in the water, which hatch as tadpoles. The tadpoles morph into frogs. Frogs shed their skin weekly. What do you think this means?

Frogs can jump very high and usually jump for their food. Frogs breathe with their nostrils and their skin. Frogs don't drink water; they absorb it through their skin. Frogs never close their eyes, even when sleeping. Each trait is symbolic. What do they say to you?

I didn't know all these facts about frogs when this memory came back to me. I simply did an internet search of frogs. It took about three minutes. Now I have a greater understanding of what frogs may represent. If I didn't research them, I would still have enough information from my knowledge about frogs, having lived on a pond, to interpret the memory. What meanings do frogs suggest to you?

Because frogs go from egg to tadpole to frogs, they would represent transformation. It can be a physical transformation. When someone sheds 100 pounds it is often called a transformation. When someone suddenly stops seeing themselves as victims and start to take responsibility for their actions that would be considered an emotional or psychological transformation. When someone has a spiritual revelation, it may propel them into a spiritual transformation. These are the different levels at which transformation can be interpreted.

Frogs also shed their skin weekly; this is another sign of transformation. When we find a snakeskin that has been shed, it would be a symbolic message to us that we are going through a transformation. Shedding skin weekly would indicate multiple transformations, a time of ongoing growth and change. At six years old I'm sure all types of transformation were occurring.

Let's not forget who crippled the frog. Cats in their positive symbolic aspect represent autonomy and healthy boundaries. In negative spiritual symbolism it's amplified, they represent selfishness, complete separation from others, from Oneness. The cat may have been reflecting a part of me that was beginning to dissociate from spirit and starting to believe the prevailing collective paradigms; at six years old I was still not fully indoctrinated. The separation paradigm I was starting to believe (cat) would prevent a part of me (frog) from jumping to the heights required to know my Divine Self. That belief in separation (cat) would keep me earthbound (symbolized by the frog losing its legs), often symbolic of being in ego. The part of us that believes it is separate from others and apart from the One Consciousness causes us suffering.

The lily pad upon which I placed the frog is the plant of the Lotus (water lily). The Lotus blossom represents enlightenment. It is a symbol of the blossoming of self-realization. We often see this symbol in our culture as we awaken collectively. When I initially wrote the description of the frog, I realized it sounded like a depiction of Buddha, the peaceful man with the big belly meditating in nature. Buddha experienced self-realization in his lifetime. The lotus flower is often associated with Buddha.

Buddha means the Awakened One. These symbols all point to enlightenment.

The fact that frogs never close their eyes points to one who sees everything. When one is enlightened, they are in the perfect knowing of Truth. They are always able to see the Truth. Metaphorically, their eyes are always open.

I poured water over the frog's head. To me, raised as a Catholic, that would represent baptism. Baptism is symbolic of the Holy Spirit entering the body, another sign of enlightenment. The Holy Spirit represents the Divine Feminine. Baptism removes sin; sin is simply the erroneous belief in separation from which all fear behavior originates. Baptism is symbolic of the initiation that brings us to Oneness.

The frog jumps for its food. We will not nurture our spirit with what is offered in the low density of this plane. We must look higher for the food that will feed our souls. Meditation and other inspirational practices will bring us to a higher frequency.

Frogs absorb water and air through their skin. Water represents being immersed in spirit. Air represents our life force, energy, our inspiration. We are surrounded by spirit, immersed in spirit, and it flows through us. Everything is Source Energy. Everything is God. When we have the symbolism of being immersed in water and air it is symbolic of being immersed in Divine Love.

It is suffering that causes us to look for another way, *the same suffering that is the scourge of our life is also our savior.* The frog had no legs. The frog suffered. It was forced into stillness. This symbolizes the part of me that knows that through stillness I will awaken. I will not transform by jumping from one place to another, from one project to another, from one drama to another, one relationship to another, or one self-help book to another. It is only when we have suffered enough and realize we need to change that we question our conditioning. We can then ask for help. After asking for help we can go into stillness so that we can receive the answer. The Holy Spirit is the bridge between us and Source Consciousness. Be Still and Know that I am God.

Why did this memory resurface now? If all is energy, and it's been well established that it is, then this memory is coming to me because I am vibrating at the same frequency as when I was six years old and found the frog sitting in the grass. This brings to my consciousness an excerpt of a poem by T. S. Elliot,

> *"We shall not cease from exploration*
> *And the end of all our exploring*
> *Will be to arrive where we started*
> *And know the place for the first time."*

The quote of Jesus from the Book of Matthew, "Verily I say unto you, unless ye be converted and become as *little children*, *ye shall* not enter into the Kingdom of Heaven." What does this mean to you? To me it says that children are uncorrupted by the collective. They are free from the lies and conditioning that eventually overtakes our lives. I believe we are born still immersed in God. We are taught separation. We are taught we must compete and compare. When we give up the illusion of separation we become as little children once again and enter the kingdom, which is not in the sky, not anywhere external to us, not in the future, not in time at all. It is us. Jesus said, "for, behold, the kingdom of God is within you" in response to the Pharisees asking when the Kingdom of God will come. It is programmed out of us by society. Become as a child and remember that you are a divine spark of the One Source of All That Is.

What does my role in this story say about me currently when the memory is resurfacing? Baptizing brings the Holy Spirit to people. It is the realization of what we have always been. In writing this book I am delivering a message of transformation, of giving up our old paradigms, beliefs, and roles. I am asking you to consider a way out of suffering. I am asking you to question everything you have ever "known." I have also asked that this book be infused with the Frequency of Love so that all who have it may receive guidance from the Holy Spirit and the Highest Good may come of it. Actual baptism, pouring water or immersion in water is a symbolic act of accepting our Divinity. When you shower, or splash water or your face, or swim, feel the joy of swimming in Divine Love. It is a reminder that you are always loved.

After I left, the frog died. We must die to our old selves, to our old beliefs to transform. The ego must surrender. The ego is simply our conditioned self, the part of us that believes in separation. Don't worry, we won't lose our sparkling personality, only our self-destructive ego self. This applies at every level. We must let go of our old beliefs and constructs so we may grow and heal physically, emotionally, and spiritually.

I don't think the six-year-old me could comprehend that a frog was a message. *All experiences and dreams reflect our lives at the time they occur.* At six years old

I was still very naïve and not greatly influenced by the outside world. My religious education was just beginning. I was fortunate, as a Catholic, to not have experienced the horror stories that some have, but to have a lovely nun as my Sunday school teacher. All I was taught was that I was loved by Jesus. Even at six years old, when most children have been almost fully conditioned, I lived in a quieter, more spacious world. I was in this collective, but still not entirely of it. I spent most of my time in the woods, at the beach, almost always near water. I was a quiet child. This message of spiritual transformation reflected my frequency at the time. I feel extremely fortunate that I had that experience and that I was able to revisit it and its implications in my current life. I now have the tools to decode it and integrate the symbolic meaning into my life.

Do you have childhood memories that pop into your mind repeatedly? Whenever you have a memory resurface, know that you are vibrating at the same frequency you were at the time of the event. What was going on at that time? How does the memory make you feel? Are there people in the memory, what do they represent to you? What other questions can you ask about the memory? In addition to examining the symbolism, try to recall if anything significant was going on in your life then. It may give you some insight as to why you are being shown this part of your life again. Explore the most memorable events of your childhood for symbolism.

CHAPTER 14

Everyone in Your Life Represents Part of You

Debbie was having a hard time with her emotions concerning her family. She was feeling left out. We probably all feel like outsiders in our own family at times. She was feeling unloved.

She stopped at the supermarket on her way home and was in the parking lot, walking to the store. In front of her was a small family. The young boy was obviously neurodivergent. He turned around, looked at Debbie and said, "Hi." Debbie gave him a big smile and returned his greeting. He turned around again and asked her what her name was. She told him it was Debbie. Then he turned to his mother and said, "She's Debbie. I love Debbie." As they walked into the store he turned around again and said, "Hi, Debbie, you're pretty." Debbie thanked him. Then she thanked the Universe for sending this little boy as a sign of how loved she is. She knew that she had just been blessed by the Christ Consciousness.

The young boy represented the part of Debbie that was innocent and pure, that wasn't ruled by ego. He represented her Divine Self, the part of her that was part of God, the part that loved her unconditionally and saw her spiritual beauty. This sign from God that she was loved was all that Debbie needed.

Don't let the actions or inactions of others define your worthiness. You are priceless, you are loved beyond your comprehension. You are more than loved, you are love itself. Let go of all expectation of being unconditionally loved by anyone in this physical realm. The ego, ruled by fear, cannot fully love anyone.

Debbie decided to ask the Holy Spirit, the Divine Feminine, for help because this issue of feeling unloved by her family was a recurring one in her emotional life. Then Debbie had a revelation: If we create everything in our life then she had created this situation. Why? What did it represent? What was her Higher Self trying to tell her? She knew what her ego was trying to tell her. Her ego was telling her she wasn't lovable and she was unimportant. Her ego wanted her to believe she was unworthy and undeserving.

If this world is really a "living dream" then she had created the whole scenario. What did her family represent in this dream? They represented the part of her that believed she was separate from Love (God). In her perceived exclusion by them her ego's belief in separation was reinforced. "Yay," thought her ego, "I have just proved to you that you are worthless, no one wants to be connected with you. To make yourself feel better let's project your insecurities onto other people and demonize them. We can be a victim and feel superior in our suffering."

Every time there is someone in your life or dreams whom you perceive to be excluding you, treating you badly, betraying you, or abandoning you, your ego is simply telling you you're unworthy. This can never be true. The ego is a liar because it lives in fear of dying, of you no longer needing it. It wants you to believe anything based in fear and insecurity.

Debbie knew she could never be separate from God. She recognized her Divinity. But, like all of us, she forgot sometimes. How can anyone be excluded from an energy that is everywhere? How can anyone be excluded from Love?

Interestingly, Debbie was going through a period of spiritual growth when this false belief that she was unloved surfaced and caused her to do a nosedive. The ego was fighting back. It didn't want her to grow and abandon it, so it presented her with an old familiar pattern to sideline her. Watch out for the ego, when we're growing it gets nervous and tries to bring us down. Congratulations on upsetting your ego; it means you're making progress!

When Debbie realized she, as her small ego self, had created the whole scenario she laughed out loud. She had created this outward symbol of her own internalized feelings of unworthiness and unimportance, of being separate and alone. She understood this was the best "lesson" she would probably ever receive as it reminded her that *everything she experienced in the physical realm in any given moment is a projection of her vibration in that moment.*

Intellectually she had known this and felt its Truth, but now on a very deep level she knew it. She then understood there is no Truth in the ego's world, only illusion. If ego only brings us lies, then we can learn to recognize ego's voice and see the truth. If ego only brings us illusion, how can we take affront from the egoic behavior of others? How can we believe the actions and attacks of the deceitful ego, whether ours or another's?

The person who appears to be attacking us is acting from ego, acting from their fears and insecurities. We experience an attack when we are in the vibration of fear, experiencing from a place of ego. The ego loves to assume, to take things personally, to be the victim. Our own fearful thoughts and beliefs caused a vibratory match with this attack and attracted it to us. The Divine Being the person who attacked us really is would never attack us but loves us always and unconditionally. The Divine Being we are would never perceive attack. Our ego perceives attack and is defensive. Whenever we feel defensive, we are in ego. It's another reason to be mindful of our emotions and reactions.

We believe ego's lies only because of our indoctrination into the world of ego. Can we give up the conditioned beliefs that cause so much pain or are they too familiar and safe for us? It's time to see the world for what it is and rejoice in our Truth. Change is a good thing.

It took Debbie years to figure it out, but most people go through their entire lives believing their programming. This challenge also reminded her our evolution is not a straight line up but a crooked staircase. It simultaneously showed her that when she humbly asks for help, she will receive it and be able to take the next step. The moment she realized it was a false ego creation, she felt unconditional love for her family and for herself.

This doesn't mean Debbie will never be hurt again by the actions of others. It does mean she's closer to that possibility and she may very well reach that point in her life. She can now be mindful of the fact that everything fearful, anxiety producing, anger provoking, all negative feelings are a construct of ego. When we are living unconsciously, what we create, the painful lesson, is our best teacher. When we are mindful of our emotions and feel ourselves going into ego, we can take a deep breath and remember we are Children of God, Divine Expressions of Love. We can remind ourselves we are always deeply loved and accepted unconditionally. At the point of uncomfortable or painful emotion we can recognize ego influence and laugh at the agony we put ourselves through. It may seem too simple, simple is not necessarily easy, but witnessing our painful emotions alerts us to a need for self-correction in our thinking and our beliefs.

If you are having an issue and the Universe sends you a loving message, like the boy who came to Debbie representing Unconditional Love, be sure to say thank you and express your gratitude for the love sent your way. Debbie believes the love message for which she was grateful prompted the Universe to send her more messages for which she would feel grateful and opened her to hearing them. Her energy of gratitude at a time of deep hurt initiated more love signs from the Universe.

The Universe reflects our thoughts and beliefs. Are yours joyful, loving, and filled with gratitude? If they are that's what you will receive, more reasons to feel joyful, loving, and grateful.

Recognize the lie of ego and recognize the only real Love is the Love of God, of the Christ Consciousness, which is in all of us and which we recognize as we are set free from the expectation of receiving love in the ego driven world.

Without the need or expectation of receiving anything real from ego there is no disappointment, no pressure to "be" anything other than your Self. You are free. And this knowing also allows others the same freedom to be themselves. Remembering who we truly are also helps others see their True Self. Remember the words of Jesus, "The Kingdom of Heaven is within." It's not outside of us. We won't find it in the "ego love" of our wounded compatriots in this collective creation of fear. True Love is inside of us and as we emanate the vibration of Love out to the world, we help to bring all beings on our planet into alignment with God.

CHAPTER 15

Body Beautiful

Our body is probably the most accurate reflection of what's going on in our emotional life. The best way to interpret the body's messages is to understand what each part of the body does. For instance, the liver removes toxins from the body. If your liver profile comes back from the lab with some red flags, it's time to figure out what toxic emotions you are holding onto that are affecting your health. Anger is a stressful toxin to the human body. The liver is almost universally considered symbolic of anger. It is where bile is produced. Bile is often used as a metaphor for anger. Are we holding on to anger and not expressing it in a healthy way. Forgiveness is the medicine to cure anger, spite, resentment, envy, and hate.

You may be very clear about why you feel angry. If we suppress our anger, it is hard to recognize we are holding it. I was completely unaware of the anger I held when I was younger. Have you been complaining a lot lately? Are you easily irritated? Do you overreact? Perhaps you are holding anger from repressed memories. Ask your

Higher Self if you are suppressing anger and what the source is. Just relax and wait for an answer.

How do we forgive? Often, the first step in forgiveness is to think of the person as a young child and ask questions. What was their life like? What happened to them to make them act in the "unforgivable" ways in which they do? If you can see them as a small child who was emotionally wounded by their caregivers, it's easier to forgive them. This is the beginning of forgiveness. It usually needs to be done over and over until the forgiveness is fully given. It is a wonderful daily practice for emotional health.

Think of all the idioms related to feet. He always lands on his feet. She tends to drag her feet. You must stand on your own two feet. He pulled the rug out from under her feet. Always keep your feet planted firmly on the ground. Don't let the grass grow under your feet. Once he got his foot in the door, he had it made. She got cold feet right before the wedding.

To me feet represent our self-awareness and our awareness of the motivation of others. When we are walking through life it's good to know where we stand.

He always lands on his feet because he understands how things work in this world. He has good self-awareness. He also understands what makes people tick. He may have developed these talents because he was oppressed as a child. Children who had to "read" a parent to know if they were safe or not from physical or verbal abuse often grow up to be exceptionally adept at reading others. This skill was a matter of emotional or physical survival for them.

Katie has chronic foot issues. She doesn't know who she is. She runs from one idea to the next, one project to the next, one relationship to the next. If she stopped to do a review and see what has given her true happiness in her life, she may see which direction would fulfill her.

Imagine this, a woman buys a farm. She walks to the edge of the field and looks out to the horizon, her feet planted firmly on the ground. This image shows me someone who knows who they are, what they want, and how to achieve it. It's a field of dreams. If we don't know what we want it's because we don't know who we are. When we know who we are, *unencumbered by our past indoctrination*, we can stand firmly on our own two feet knowing what we want and how to get it. Step from conditioned to conscious.

What do our knees do? They bend. They give us flexibility. They allow us to change course easily if we need to. Our knees are about being flexible and going with the flow. If we're having problems with our knees, we might look for ways in which we are inflexible. Are we stubborn and prideful at times? Do we hate it when we are in a situation where we don't feel in control? Does it throw us off to have plans suddenly change or to be asked to do something unplanned?

When people have knee problems it's an indication that they may have had a very erratic childhood. Their parent's behavior was probably very inconsistent. A child who grows up in chaos craves control.

With this need to control we stubbornly hold onto beliefs. We may also stubbornly hold onto routine. We may be inflexible with our time. Our safety feels very tenuous and any change in routine or behavior brings back our old feelings of anxiety and pain.

Roger had chronic knee stiffness and pain. He would sometimes get a call from his wife when he was on his way home from work asking him to pick up milk at the convenience store. She stopped calling him because he refused to stop as he "hadn't planned on it."

Growing up Roger never knew what his father's mood might be or whether he would be the target of his father's alcohol induced rages. His father would humiliate him and berate him, often in public. Feeling powerless as a child, he needed to be in total control as an adult to feel safe. Unfortunately, it had the opposite effect as his need for control drove others away. Holding onto unconscious behaviors based in fear only hurts us.

One way to start living a more flexible life is to use the words potential, possible, consider, and could more often. It's possible this will work. I don't need to control this situation; the world won't end if I compromise. That idea has potential, let's consider it. I'll consider what you said before I respond. It's possible I'm wrong. We could try that.

Be flexible, be open to new ideas and experiences. It could lead to amazing possibilities.

Our hips are what determines our stride. They are all about forward motion. When we have hip issues it may be an indication that we are stagnant, in a rut. We may have lost our passion or fear failure, for whatever reason we aren't progressing on our authentic path. Look at your goals and dreams, are you moving closer, or have you put them aside with some rationalization about why you can't proceed right now? Don't give up on your dreams. Move forward.

He carried the weight of the world on his shoulders. She shouldered the responsibility. He had broad shoulders. She was a shoulder to cry on. They stood on the shoulders of those who had gone before them.

These idioms are about responsibility. We all have burdens, but how do we shoulder them. Do we carry them with a sense of earnest and loving service to others or with resentment and anger? Shoulder problems are caused by erroneous beliefs about our responsibilities.

In families there is often one person who carries too much of the responsibility, they may be overburdened. One person may do all the cooking, cleaning, and caring while also working full time. If this sounds like you, it's time to rewrite the nonverbal contract. Let others know that you will not take their responsibilities. Don't be a martyr. When we say, "I do everything around here," it is usually in the form of complaint and the ego loves to complain. It makes the ego feel superior. I'm better because I take care of everyone, no one takes care of me, I'm the victim here. Complaining is the ego's form of fun.

Rather than doing everything and resenting it, work on an equitable solution. Children are doing less and less in the way of chores, even though studies show that children who have responsibilities at home are more well-adjusted, happier, and have better self-esteem. Contributing adds to their sense of worth and connection with their family. If your children are unable to help, try enlisting the help of family, friends, or community. No one is an island. Allow others to help you. You are worthy of help. You have permission to ask for help. You can even ask your Higher Self and help will be sent.

At work do we look for approval from our "superiors" by doing more work, putting in the extra hours, and end up living an unbalanced life? Then when the boss overlooks you or underappreciates your contribution you become resentful and angry. If you can do your job well without expectation of praise and keep a healthy personal/career balance, you may find that you no longer have shoulder issues.

Did your parents give you chores? Were they unreasonable in their expectations of your abilities? Did you feel burdened as a child by your responsibilities? Were you the parentified child, often taking care of your parents in emotional or physical ways and taking over their responsibilities? It's important to give children some responsibility, but their job as children is mostly to play and experience new things. If you were overburdened as a child, you may have carried the belief that all responsibility is a chore and there's no time for play.

As adults who experienced this, we are often looking for what people want from us, we don't believe we deserve love just for being. This belief holds us in a specific energetic vibration, and we attract more people who are users, who want something from us, reinforcing our belief we aren't valuable as we are but only for what we provide. You don't have to do anything to prove your value. Claim your inherent worthiness. You are important.

Take time to play as an adult. Having fun with our family while completing chores is a good way to model to our children that life's daily work doesn't have to be a chore and we can enjoy it. Sing and dance through chores. A spoonful of sugar helps the medicine go down.

Giving up what no longer serves us helps to lighten our load. Do you really need a perfectly manicured lawn? Grow a carefree pollinator garden instead. Do you really need a perfect home? Let the dust collect a little longer. Do you really need all the busyness and all the chores? Can you let some go? Let go of the expectations of a perfect life and stop caring what others think of you. When we give ourselves a break and don't need to prove anything to others we also give them permission to let go of unnecessary work. Let go of tasks that don't benefit you or your family. Let go of the burdens.

Our gut symbolizes our intuition. We are often told we should go with our gut feelings, but, contrarily, children are constantly told what to do while their feelings and intuition aren't considered. When a child has a stomachache, I would suggest that they have tried to follow their intuition but have been thwarted on all sides. Their gut instincts are being denied. If they don't follow what their gut tells them verses what they are being told to do, the conflict materializes as "gut" pain. When a child has a stomachache, they are having a reaction to external authorities or prevailing norms, forcing them to behave in ways that are incongruent with their gut feelings.

Children often get stomachaches right before heading out the door to school. At school they are told how to behave, how to think, how to interact, what to believe... They are not allowed to be who they are except for those few minutes of recess where they are monitored. The older they get the more those breaks are filled with peer pressure. Children need more encouragement to do what they want, to color outside the lines, to think outside the box, to dream outside the collective social paradigms. They need unstructured play time outdoors.

The next time a child tells you they have a stomach-ache perhaps you'll be able to identify their conflict. Let them know they are perfect just as they are. Let them know they really can trust their gut. Explain to them that if they have a belly ache it might mean they are doing something or being asked to do something that doesn't feel right to them. Children can be taught it's okay to not agree with authority figures and to question what feels wrong to them. This claim of self-authority by the child doesn't condone disrespect; it celebrates self-respect.

Assure them if it feels uncomfortable talking with a teacher or other authority figure about doing some-thing they don't feel comfortable with, they can wait and discuss it with you. Children need validation that their intuition holds great value. We're not talking about sex-ual abuse here. Every child needs to be safe and should know they hold sovereign power over their bodies.

We've heard some people use the expression, "That took guts." They refer to someone who did the right thing even though they were doing something outside the norm or it put them in conflict. It is often used in ref-erence to bucking the establishment, in any of its many forms. It takes guts to be a free thinker in a brainwashed culture. It takes guts to live a life that brings you joy. It takes guts to be an individual. It takes guts to live outside the box and not be "normal." But it's worth it.

If you have chronic "gut" issues, then you've prob-ably been suppressing your authentic self for some time. It's a very crowded club. That may be why antacids are one of the most commonly used over the counter drugs in the industrialized world.

As a child were you taught to suppress who you are to conform? It happens so often that eventually we can't even hear our intuition anymore. Start to bring it back by asking for your intuition to return. It is a part of you after all. You'll start to hear that wise voice when you quiet your mind. If you get a stomachache, ask yourself if you've been denying your intuition by doing something that just doesn't seem right, that doesn't sit quietly with you. Take back your power. Who cares what other people think? Not you!

She has a hand in everything. All hands on deck. He's very handy. She's got her hands full. Can you give me a hand? His drinking got out of hand. My hands are tied. Try your hand at this.

These idioms are about doing. The following idioms are about giving and receiving.

He always had his hand out. He handed over his paycheck every week. Don't bite the hand that feeds you. The property changed hands. Hand me downs.

The symbolism of hands may seem very broad, but it really isn't as complex as it first appears. We all know that hands are for doing. We do almost everything with our hands. Hands also give and receive.

Ruth broke her right hand; this incident signifies doing as the main symbolism, as the right side of the body represents the masculine yang energy which is about action. If it was the left hand she broke, it would have been about giving and receiving, which is the left-sided feminine yin principle.

Ruth kept constantly busy. If we fill our lives with activity, it is usually because we are avoiding something. That something is often emotional issues from our past preventing us from living our best life. Issues with the right hand mean it's time to stop doing so much and figure out what we are avoiding. Then we can start doing what we love, fulfill a dream we've been afraid of pursuing, be ourselves.

If we have issues with our left hand, it will signify giving and receiving, not doing. Do you give with an open heart? Are you generous? Were you taught as a child that there wasn't enough and now you can't give without feeling you will be left with less? Do you allow others to give to you? As a child, were you treated generously? Were you the one who didn't have what the other kids had? You may have internalized the belief you don't deserve what others have. You may have been raised with a belief in lack. When someone gives you a present or a compliment can you accept graciously?

When dealing with hand issues look at what you were taught as a child about doing, giving, and receiving. Claim a new truth.

There is probably no part of the human anatomy presented to us more poetically than the heart. The symbolism of the heart is probably the most universal of all our body parts. The Heart tells us how we feel. The heart speaks of tenderness and compassion. It is the symbol of our love and connection. We give our heart to our Beloved. We wear our heart on our sleeve. We can be open hearted by being courageous and vulnerable or we may be hard hearted or cold hearted.

A heart attack occurs when an artery that brings blood to the heart muscle becomes blocked. The blood, which represents joy, is unable to get to the heart muscle and it seizes up. The heart represents love, connectedness to others, and life. A heart blockage symbolizes placing a metaphorical wall (blockage) around the heart to protect it. This wall may keep someone from being hurt emotionally, but it also prevents them from living a life full of love and joy. They are so afraid of getting hurt they miss out on opportunities for connection. And this lack of intimacy is what ultimately causes the heart attack.

To experience love and joy we need to be vulnerable and take emotional risks. Avoiding pain increases the pain of isolation and loneliness.

Heart issues may directly relate to a fear of intimacy, vulnerability, trust, and devotion. Was affection given freely in our birth family? Did our parents disappoint us over and over by not accepting us as who we were? Have we had repeated relationships as adults that ended in hurt and disappointment because of the birth family dysfunction we internalized? Did we become bitter and hardhearted, or hurt and brokenhearted? We learn what love is from our birth family and if "love" was painful we choose unhealthy, painful relationships.

Some people with heart issues may have had many opportunities to experience love and joy in their lives, but because they had indoctrinated beliefs that they were unworthy they stayed in the familiar pattern of choosing partners who were incapable of seeing their worthiness. Emotionally healthy people don't go into relationship with unhealthy people.

Heart attacks may also be related to blocking our emotions, keeping them pushed down until they explode. We can learn to deal with our anger, our hurt, and realize we can get through any emotional turmoil with support, forgiveness, and Love.

Love is the answer when it comes to the heart. Accept yourself as worthy and lovable. Don't let the stories other people told you about who you are determine who you believe you are. You are important and valued. Love yourself as God loves you, fully and unconditionally.

Do you have pain or issues with certain areas of your body? Whatever part of the body that is having an issue can be examined for the symbolic meaning. What does that organ do? What does that joint do? What does the disease represent? Diabetes is an inability to metabolize sugar. What does that mean to you? Cancer is an unhealthy proliferation of mutant cells, what does that mean to you? In what area of the body did the cancer start? What does the thyroid gland do? What is the point of the little toe? The answers that ring true for you, that make you say, "Aha," are the answers the universe wants you to see. Ask questions for any type of symbolism and get your very special and personal answer.

CHAPTER 16

I Should be Committed

I was unexpectedly invited to a wedding. The mother of the bride and I had recently developed a friendship. When the wedding was planned we were just getting to know each other but months later we were close friends. When a friend of hers who planned on attending the wedding had to cancel at the last minute, she invited me, and I happily accepted.

About halfway home I decided to turn on the car radio, which was set to a classical station. Mendelssohn's Wedding March from A Midsummer Night's Dream was playing, and it was the most familiar part of the wedding march, Bom bom bom bom bom bom bom ~ Bom bom bom bom bom bom.... I might have taken this synchronicity of events to mean that I would soon be meeting someone and starting a long-term relationship.

Except, a few weeks before going to the wedding, I had the first in this series of symchronicities. I signed up for a spiritual class. The teacher walked to the front and stood quietly for a few minutes before starting the class.

At that moment I felt an energetic wedding ring on my left ring finger. It felt like energy encircling my finger. That's really the only way to describe it.

I knew this didn't mean I would marry this man. At first, I thought it might be an indication that I was ready for a long-term relationship, but the coincidence of the timing (being at a spiritual teaching) discounted that for me, it didn't "ring" true. I was curious as to what it really meant.

So, what did the energetic wedding ring mean? A wedding ring is about commitment. I felt the ring when a spiritual teacher stood ready to teach. I believe I was being asked if I was ready to commit wholly (holy) to my spiritual path. Nuns and priests wear wedding rings as a symbolic reminder of their commitment to God.

Look at the different meanings of the word ring. A wedding ring binds people together; it is a symbol of eternal connection. A ring is a circle which encompasses everything; it is the beginning and the end. A ring is also a sound, it resonates, as in the ringing of a bell. It is a vibration. A church usually has a steeple or bell tower. The steeple symbolizes aspiring toward heaven. The bell rings for the members to come to service. The beautiful pealing of the church bells on Sunday morning represents the vibration of God calling you to Love, calling you to Sacred Service. The One Consciousness, in its Divine Knowing, has created these symbols. When we bring symbols to consciousness, we recognize direction from our Higher Self.

A wedding ring is a call for commitment. I am being told to commit to being a spiritual student and teacher. Through writing this book I am fulfilling part of my commitment to both paths as I am using this book to teach as well as learning a lot in the process. Much of this book was inspired.

These three symbols ~ a spontaneous invitation to a wedding, hearing Mendelssohn's Wedding March, and feeling an energetic wedding ring at a spiritual teaching are directing me to make a commitment to serving the Highest Good.

CHAPTER 17

Lucid Dreaming

Lucid Dreaming is experienced when we are having a sleeping dream and during the dream we realize that we are dreaming. At this point we can take control of the dream and make it go in any direction we want.

My dream started with me running for my life through corridors that went on like a maze. I was in a science laboratory of some kind, a research building. A monster was chasing me. I didn't know what kind of monster, but I knew it was big and would kill me if it caught up with me. I ran through the hallways looking for a way out. I was absolutely panicked.

I burst out of a hallway and found myself on the second-floor balcony of an immense lobby. The entire front wall of it was glass and overlooked a forest. I could see green treetops to the horizon. I knew the monster would be there any moment. Paralyzed with fear, I suddenly realized I was dreaming. It became crystal clear to me I could do anything I wanted. I could fly off this balcony, crash through the glass, and soar safely away over the green forest. And that is exactly what I did. I felt joyously free, completely fulfilled, whole and happy flying to my freedom. End of dream.

Let's deconstruct this dream. Where did it take place? A Science/Research Building. What does this mean to you? What does science make you think of? To me the building was very impersonal, sterile, certainly not a cozy place. It represents a world where everything has a logical explanation, is quantifiable and qualifiable. It is the building in which scientists prove or disprove theories based only in the five senses. To me it would represent a limited exploration of what is. We are so much more than what we can comprehend with our five senses.

In research labs the rooms are filled with scientists who are determining for society what is true and what is not. In these facilities nothing is deemed real unless it can be quantifiable. They are constructing our belief systems. I was trying to get out of a place that was trying to tell me what was true based on a limited view of the universe.

The hallways went on like a maze with many closed doors. What do we usually find in mazes? Rats. Rats being taught how to get to the reward in the most direct way. I ran through the halls never knowing which way to go, which turn to take? Do I want to fit into the established pattern and compete with others for the fastest time to the reward? Do I even want the reward being offered? I never saw the monster. Was it real? Is the monster a part of me? The part of me so fearful it wants to take the easy path of conformity and acceptance in a society that measures success by attainment in the physical world rather than through personal fulfillment and happiness. Is the monster my ego?

The part of me which is running from the monster is trying to break the ties with that limited quantified world. It wants to rise above physical limitations and paradigms and see beyond what can be seen under a microscope or in a social experiment.

My interpretation of this dream, after asking myself about each aspect of it, is that for my entire life I was being trained to get to the reward. Maybe the reward was the American Dream, maybe it was something else I hadn't consciously chosen, some collective construct that fit nicely with my assigned roles.

The Monster would represent the part of me that adopted the personal, social, and cultural norms of my upbringing. The monster suggests that everything I am is measurable, can be given a label. The monster tells me I am defined by standards that lack creativity, potential, high vibration, and my ability to Love and employ free will. The monster represents the part of me that believes I am far less than I am. To the monster I am just another lab rat running in a maze. I am far more than that, truly. Like you, I am a creative spark of God.

I was running from the part of me that believed I had to conform to be safe and accepted. According to this symbol of societal norms if I didn't follow the same route as everyone else I would be devoured in a world that allows little tolerance for personal expression. I didn't need to fear the monster; it didn't exist except in my unconscious, programmed belief system. That is why it was invisible in the dream. It is the illusion. It has nothing to do with me.

The lobby represented a way out, finally, but isn't a lobby the way in? Here we are again.

"We shall not cease from exploration, and the end of all our exploring will be to arrive where we started and know the place for the first time.» - T. S. Eliot

We come from spirit, and we will return to spirit. What brought me back to the light, to spirit? Panic. The threat of untold suffering. Without the threat I wouldn't have "woken up" in my dream. My desperation drove me to "awaken." Suffering in our daily lives propels us to awaken. It makes us ask the question, "Is that all there is?" Suffering is our call to change, to stop settling, to stop being what we are not. We've had enough.

Monsters are of our own making. My dream tells me that I have a fear of living a life of ego identification. My unconscious belief that I need to conform to fit in was the monster. The part of us that strives to fit in is the part of us killing us, killing our potential and creative spark, crushing our dreams, suppressing our soul. We thrive when we are open and free enough to be creative, to love, to expand, and to experience joy, to be authentic.

What was behind the doors? More people living compact prescribed lives? Or were these doors filled with amazing experiences we would never know if our focus was to get through the maze in the fastest time, running ahead of our ego? If this was your dream, what do you think is behind the closed doors?

When I became aware I was in a dream, I took complete control. I flew, crashing through the glass and soaring over a never-ending forest of green. Green is the color of Springtime, of rebirth and renewal. This was telling me I could be reborn and follow the path of the Awakened Self. Green is also the color of the Heart Chakra. I can follow my Heart's desire. The Heart Chakra is about expansion, love, passion and compassion, desire, and fulfillment. The heart chakra connects the lower three chakras of the physical/emotional self with the higher three chakras of the Spiritual Self. It connects heaven and earth. This connection allows us to see who we are and what we can do when we live in Consciousness. This was a liberating dream for me. I have never felt such a sense of freedom before.

Take this dream and make it yours. You can leave behind your ego identification, your programming, and be you. Don't be part of the Control Group, be the Variable!

CHAPTER 18

Addiction

Addictions hinder our emotional maturing process. Have you ever known someone who started drinking or doing drugs in high school and never stopped? If you have interacted with them recently you may also have noticed that they've never changed. They are still having the same conversations and hold the same belief system they had at the time they began their substance abuse. They found it too frightening and too overwhelming to face their emotional pain, so they chose an escape vehicle and haven't stopped driving it.

When we avoid dealing with our "wounded child" self we wallow in our victimhood, believing the outside world is attacking us. Only when we have done the work of self-discovery will we recognize our power and take responsibility. The escape vehicle of choice whether work, alcohol, money, shopping, drugs, sex, food, diet, exercise, etc., is an impediment to our growth and growth is crucial to leaving addiction and walking away as a healthy, self-aware human being. It's a seemingly insurmountable paradox. If we are brave enough to upset the precarious balance in which we exist and trust that the pain of our past won't kill us, we can move forward.

Our childhood might give us the keys to unlock the emotional pain behind our addictions. If we don't remember our childhood, we can surmise from our addiction that it wasn't good for us. We can conclude we were not given the nurturing and love we needed. Most people with addictions feel unworthy; they believe they are not good enough. Doing the work, realizing we are not the unlovable, unworthy person we have been programmed to believe is the only way to overcome addiction. Taking full responsibility for our addiction is important. Blaming justifies a belief our addiction is someone else's fault and therefore we are the victim and can't control it. Forgiveness gives us back our power.

A person with addiction will continue to get worse and the addiction and emotional turmoil will escalate until they finally have the courage to dive into the deep, bring the old wounds up to the surface and heal/deal with them. It can be done voluntarily or the person who is addicted can wait for their lives to explode and force them to deal with it. Some may choose to die rather than face their past and the consequential feelings of unworthiness, self-hate, blame, and shame. Bring the erroneous beliefs to light and you can work on discarding them as what they are, trash.

Valerie's father abandoned her when she was a toddler. Even though he lived in the same city he rarely saw her, sometimes going for years without so much as a birthday card or phone call. She started drinking in high school.

As a young adult she got a tattoo on her back. It was a tattoo of the Egyptian God Osiris. She had no idea who this God was when she got the tattoo. Osiris is one of the Egyptian father Gods. She was carrying her father on her back. She needed to be real about her feelings concerning her father's neglect. She still subconsciously internalized that it was because she was unimportant and unworthy. She chose relationships with men who didn't value her. And she continued to drink.

On her father's birthday one year she invited him to join her family for dinner and cake. She spent the day cooking. He called to tell her he wouldn't be coming due to a car issue. She offered to pick him up, but he declined.

When her mother walked in, she was sobbing. Valerie told her it was because she wasted her whole day cooking when could have been doing other things. With that phone call she was reminded of how unimportant she was to him. She experienced five-year old Valerie waiting for him to show up like he promised and once again leaving her waiting alone, feeling unwanted and unworthy. She attributed her tears to wasted time. The only time she was wasting was in trying to get a loving response from her father. He was incapable of giving her the love and attention she needed as a child and that she continued to look for as an adult. When she could finally see she was worthy, whether her father knew it or not, she would be free.

As long as she continued drinking she would suppress her feelings. She needed to stop drinking to be awake and aware enough to consciously examine her feelings, to see that her father's treatment of her reflected his wounds and had nothing to do with her. It takes courage to face our emotions, but the pain of confronting them won't kill us. It will, indeed, make us stronger.

Valerie's mother had her own issues with self-worth from her birth family conditioning. This reinforced Valerie's feelings of unworthiness. Children don't learn their self-worth from words and actions alone. They identify with their parents and if their parents feel unworthy the children "know" through extension they are also unworthy. Emotional trauma is passed down from generation to generation. We are one of the first generations in the western world blessed with the tools and insights from great teachers to help us overcome our past and stop the cycle of fear and pain. If we do the work, our children and grandchildren can have a happier, healthier life. We are our children's first and most formative teachers and models of self-worth and self-love. Do you value yourself? Do you treat yourself with love and respect? Do you take care of yourself? Do you allow others to disrespect you or treat you as worthless? What do you want to model for your children?

If Valerie could see what a truly wonderful person she is and that her father's treatment of her and her mother's personal belief in her own unworthiness speak to their wounds and not to her worthiness. If she could recognize she is inherently worthy and fully loved, she would be liberated. She can also keep in mind their behavior doesn't speak to their worthiness and lovableness either. Let's try to see everyone as the whole and holy beings they are.

Valerie needed to deal with her feelings of unworthiness, she can realize she doesn't have to carry her pain on her back for the rest of her life. A tattoo may be permanent, but her pain doesn't need to be a life sentence. Osiris also represents power, strength, and rebirth. Valerie began to look at the tattoo as a symbol of her strength and power, of her ability to transform her life. She is on her journey to self-love and wholeness.

The reason many substance abusers die from liver failure is because the liver represents anger and anger is a big factor in addiction. Anger and resentment can lead to addiction. Anger is the emotion that comes from hurt and pain. Often people with addiction blame one or both of their parents. They excuse their addiction with the rationalization that their parents were terrible to them and wounded them deeply. The paradox here is that though they excuse their own behavior blaming it on their childhood treatment, they refuse to see their parents' wounds or excuse them for their conditioned behavior.

When we can stop blaming others, let go of the anger, and forgive we will start to heal. All of us must take responsibility for our lives. All of us need to let go of blame. When we forgive others, we forgive ourselves. When we stop taking what our parents said or did to us as personal assaults, we can stop the old story and begin a new chapter. Let's sit quietly for a moment with the words of Ram Dass, "We're all just walking each other home." It's such a lovely and loving way of saying we're all doing our best. Let's love, encourage, and support each other.

Smoking cigarettes is about anger. Some symbols of anger are fire, heat, steam, etc. Cigarettes burn. When we inhale smoke, we are symbolically swallowing our anger. That's one of the reasons it's so hard to quit addictions. Whenever people try to quit cigarettes or most substances they go through periods of extreme irritability, anger, and anxiety. Instead of swallowing our anger symbolically with cigarettes and other substances we need to find a way to deal with our pain that isn't self-destructive. When working to end addiction it may be necessary to get help to recognize and deal with the hurt and anger that arises.

To begin to deal with anger we must identify it as an issue. Feel the anger, hurt, and resentment, and then begin to let go and forgive. It sounds so much easier than it is, but it's worth healing those old wounds for the peace of mind it will bring. When you feel anger or anxiety arising try to be present with it. You can't really stop the emotion, so watch it. If we aren't witnessing the emotion, then we are swimming in the emotion and we think it is us. As us it hurts. When witnessing emotions they loses some of their power. Observe yourself when you begin to feel overcome with emotion. Watch your thoughts. Be a curious onlooker.

If you have quit smoking and suddenly you have a strong desire for a cigarette (or any addictive response), look at what triggered the impulse. Take a few deep, calming breaths. Something just happened, a thought just popped into your mind, someone said or did something, an old pain resurfaced triggering your craving for a cigarette. Use deep breathing exercises to help you remain present and alert instead of diving into the emotion and the addiction. Focus on breathing and watching. Can you identify the trigger? Even if you can't, focusing on breathing can help.

With these addictions we can see the symbolism of swallowing our emotions, whether it's marijuana, cigarettes, alcohol, or drugs we start the addiction with the symbolic swallowing of emotional pain and anger.

Intravenous drug addiction has its own symbolism. We talked about blood symbolizing joy. Think of the expression, "his art is his life blood." It means it feeds his passion and brings him joy. Addicts who shoot up are trying to put some joy into their lives. They are putting drugs into their bloodstream, symbolically hoping to bring joy into their lives or at the very least escape from the pain.

I know an addict who was filled with enthusiasm when they were younger, just overflowing with life, but circumstances took a bad turn for them. They couldn't cope and developed an addiction to heroin. If they understood that nothing they experienced as children was personal, that the way they have been treated has to do with the wounds of the person who they perceive caused their pain, they could return to joy and inspiration.

Some will read this and still feel that they are not responsible because their addiction was the result of how they were treated. They believe because they were traumatized they have no control over their actions. When we realize the negative treatment we received was born of someone else's suffering and had nothing to do with us we can move forward without taking it personally, without feeling hurt and helpless. Knowing that our parents do the best they can from their own feelings of unworthiness and pain helps us to see that they are as much a victim of their ancestral heritage as we are. Rather than blaming we can now realize that we are not better or worse than anyone else. Hurt people hurt people. It's an adage that holds true. When we blame others, we can't forgive. Until we can forgive, we play the victim. It's up to us to decide how we want to proceed. We are all doing the best we can.

Being a workaholic doesn't seem to fit into the symbol of swallowing anger or suppressing emotional pain. In western society some consider being a workaholic a good thing, labeled as ambitious or motivated, but like anything else when taken to extremes it becomes unhealthy. It is a diverting technique to keep one from looking at their life and dealing with wounds from the past. It is too painful to dive deep into the subconscious and so they keep ever busy, busy, busy to avoid the inevitable thoughts and anxiety that come in a static moment. Most workaholics have another addiction, also, but they function well in the physical world. If there is a quiet moment, they fill it with their substance of choice.

What about money, how is money an addiction? Look at ways in which a drug addict will steal from friends and family to be able to buy their drugs. The addiction trumps morals. Like a drug addict, people who are addicted to money will connive to get money from people. Frequently we see families torn apart over their inheritance. Usually, a family member addicted to money will try to get more than the rest. They will make excuses or come up with erroneous reasons why they deserve more.

Because of their childhood wounds people addicted to money have no sense of self-worth. Society often indoctrinates us with the concept that the more money we make the more valuable we are. People addicted to money need to prove their importance, their worth, their very right to be here. Unless their bank account is overflowing they feel worthless, threatened, and fearful. They use status symbols to prove their worth to the world, from designer fashion to vacations, cars, and houses. It's all about presentation. It gives them a feeling of power. Money symbolizes approval, acceptance, and even love to them.

Think about billionaires that want more and more. They could never spend all the money they have, yet it's not enough. They are too addicted to money to give any away to those who live in poverty, to children dying, or to help communities, unless a tax write off is involved and it serves them financially. Their addiction to money takes away their connection to others and their compassion for others just as much as addictive drugs do. Don't expect rational behavior from someone with addiction. Their addiction speaks for them.

Anger, emotional pain, and addiction often follow a childhood without consequences. If a child is raised to believe they are superior, that the rules don't apply to them, that they can do whatever they want without negative consequences it causes them to internalize the belief that whatever they do is acceptable. They have an elitist, entitled mindset. When they leave the nest, they find there are ramifications in the outside world to their actions. They become angry when everything isn't being given to them. Because of their upbringing they will blame others for their failures and deny their own responsibility. Why would they believe anything was their fault, they were never held accountable for their actions before?

The other side of this is that they have poor self-esteem because they have been praised since childhood without any substantive action on their part. They are told how wonderful, how smart, how beautiful, how deserving, and worthy they are their whole lives, never having done anything to merit the praise.

As they mature, they see others following passions and meeting goals. They see others involved in pursuits, receiving recognition and feeling satisfaction for a job well done while they have always received the mantle of superiority for no reason other than their existence in a certain family, culture, or class. This often leads to self-loathing because they subconsciously believe that they don't deserve any of the praise and rewards. It's hard to live with self-hate so they demonize others to prove their worthiness and legitimize their elite status. They project their self-hate onto others. They are right that they do deserve abundance. Their misconception is that they deserve it more than others.

The 12 step programs are an excellent source of help to overcome addiction due to their emphasis on a Higher Power, humility, making amends, and forgiveness. I would recommend any try it, even if they don't believe in a Higher Power. They can choose to call their Higher Power the part of them that makes good and healthy decisions. It can be seen as the part of us that wants to live consciously. If an addict can admit what they have been doing isn't working and surrender to any power other than their ego, they stand a chance. They need support and love.

Most of us have heard about the experiment in which rats were put into a cage alone and had the choice to either drink from a bottle that contained plain water or a bottle that contained water mixed with a highly addictive drug. The rats had an almost 100% addiction rate to the drugged water.

Years later, Bruce Alexander, a professor of psychology in Vancouver looked at the study and saw what he determined was a glaring flaw. He decided to do his own study in which he set up what he called a "rat park." This rat park had tunnels, activities, and many rats. The rats had friends, sexual partners, community, things to do, and they enjoyed their lives. Alexander placed the two bottles, one plain water and one with drug-laced water in the rat park. The rats almost never drank from the drug water. There was close to a 0% addiction rate.

In translating this to human happiness, we must question whether addiction is due to the chemical reactions in the brain or whether it is due to feelings of disconnection. Is addiction due to a lack of acceptance of who we are? Is it due to a lack of purpose? Did we feel loved and nurtured as children? Did we feel abandoned or unsafe as children? Did our parents neglect us in favor of a sibling, career, or social life? Were we abused, verbally, physically, or sexually? Were we put on a pedestal that we couldn't justify? Many who turn to addiction feel isolated and unloved and the addiction often results in more isolation. Most friends eventually turn their backs on someone with addiction. The only friends left are their peers in addiction.

People with socially unacceptable addiction feel more and more unworthy of love and community as their lifestyle continues. They live with great shame surrounding their addiction and our society furthers those feelings with its disdain. I am not an expert on addiction, but it seems to me that embracing them, giving them love and acceptance, is an important, if not the most important, aspect of their recovery.

In 2001 Portugal had one of the worst drug problems in Europe. A panel of doctors, social workers, and psychologists met to discuss alternative ways to deal with the massive drug issues because the system they had of criminalization wasn't working. They decided to decriminalize all drugs including heroin and cocaine.

Since then, their drug addiction rates have dropped by 50%, the drug related AIDs rate dropped by 90%, the drug related imprisonment rate fell from 44% to 21%. The drug addiction rate continues to decline every year.

The government of Portugal is quick to point out that decriminalization is not necessarily the prime reason for the decline in drug addiction and the many problems associated with it. They simultaneously started social programs to support those addicted to drugs, along with job training, loans for small businesses, counseling, community programs, and social acceptance. Recognizing drug addiction as a health and psychological problem and not a criminal problem has significantly turned the tide in Portugal. It has improved not only their country, but the lives of thousands of addicts and their families. Fully one percent of citizens of Portugal were heroin addicts when this program was initiated.

Love, compassion, purpose, and community can help solve addiction issues. If you have addiction issues look to your programming. Stop believing you are less than others because you have an issue with addiction. Stop believing the indoctrination that you are unworthy of love, are a waste of space, and that you don't matter. You are a beautiful and magnificent person no matter what you have been led to believe.

I believe this is a good time to talk about codependence as there is no situation that exemplifies it more than the relationship between an addict and their caregiver, whether parent, partner, sibling, or friend. In the addiction codependence model the addict takes no responsibility. The caregiver takes all the responsibility and with it the power in the relationship.

The caregiver is in charge. The addict resents giving up their power, but the addiction is stronger than their drive to take back their power. The caregiver, on an unconscious level, may like the position they are in as it feeds a need to be a savior, to be in control, or to be superior.

A mother I know had an addicted adult child. She took her grandchildren most of the time, bought her son whatever he needed, constantly worried about him, got him into rehab multiple times, and basically took over his life. The irony here is he blamed his mother for everything wrong in his life. He believed he was a victim of his mother's verbal abuse and rage. He insisted his mother was the cause of his addiction.

The addict couldn't see that his mother, when raising him, was doing everything from a place of her own childhood wounds. He expected his mother to rise above her childhood wounds and be a good parent while he wouldn't even consider he could rise above his own childhood wounds and be a good parent to his children and give up his addiction. He expected his mother to be perfect but expected nothing from himself. He would verbally say he took full responsibility for his addiction and in the next breath blame his mother for his problems.

This reinforces the fact we cannot hold anyone but ourselves accountable for our lives. If everyone comes from a wounded place than no one can function on the level needed to raise perfectly healthy children. Some do better than others, no doubt, but we all have wounds. Some people are too wounded to meet any of their children's needs. As parents who do the emotional work we can recognize where we can do better with our children or where we went wrong with our children, but we shouldn't live in shame and blame. We realize we did the best we could and let our children know we realize we made mistakes, we acted from a place of pain and our own childhood wounds. We can let them know we love them, we are sorry, and we will do better. We can reinforce that if we treated them in a manner that didn't feel loving it was because we weren't whole enough to give them the unconditional love they deserved. Heartfelt apologies can make a big difference in healing our relationships with our children.

People with addiction must release others from the responsibility for their happiness. They may never get the apologies or validation of their mistreatment from their parents and can't depend on that for their recovery. External circumstances will never bring us happiness.

Our happiness can only come from our belief in our inherent worthiness.

Fear of lack runs most of the world. The fear is either we are lacking in resources or we lack worthiness. Once we see we are worthy our lives change in dramatic ways. Abundance and happiness come to us when we know we are worthy. It's a vibrational match.

Do you drink, smoke, shop, or fall into any of the actions that say "I'm not enough"? Is it a response to stress? Has it become a habituated response to constant stress? Don't swallow your feelings. Observe them. See them as an onlooker. I read a statistic that 37% of Americans are alcoholics. When I tell people this, most of them say they think the percentage is higher. This is clearly representative of the skewed priorities of our culture. We don't need more money or more things. We need more connection, more love, more forgiveness, more nurturing.

Let's start with forgiveness and grow from there.

CHAPTER 19

Deer Me

Carol was taking a trip with her boyfriend and his mother to visit relatives in New Jersey. Carol's boyfriend usually did the bulk of the driving, but this time he asked Carol to take the first leg of the journey. He told her to get on a certain route and then stay on it. He fell asleep.

After a few hours the route didn't look familiar to Carol. Instead of seeing the usual cities, refineries, shopping centers, and strip malls that marked the trip she was seeing woods and parks, farms and rivers. She saw deer standing in the woods watching the road or lying in the woods just relaxing. She woke up her boyfriend knowing they weren't heading to New Jersey anymore.

He was furious. They were hours out of their way now. Carol defended herself stating that if she had been given the right directions they wouldn't be here, but he wasn't taking any responsibility for the mistake. He even went so far as to call her stupid.

They turned around and eventually got back to the missed exit and the usual route of the smokestacks and swamps they were used to seeing on the interstate.

Ironically, at one point her boyfriend tried to take a shortcut due to heavy traffic and ended up getting lost in New York City.

After the trip Carol thought about the different feelings she experienced between her drive and her boyfriend's drive. To her the deer featured prominently on her route. What aspect of herself did they represent? What do deer represent to you? What feelings do they conjure? The word deer can have two meanings. It is an animal, but change the spelling and it is dear. Symbolically, on the route she took she was seeing things that were "dear" to her, nature, forests, farms, rivers, meadows, all parts of a bucolic countryside, all symbols of a simple and slower life. Deer are known for their beauty and grace. The meaning of grace is blessing. Her route brought her blessings. Deer are known to be gentle and soulful. Just look into a doe's soft brown eyes and you see the innocence and depth of them. Carol saw mainly does, which would signify the feminine, the nurturing and open aspect of herself. This is also the side of herself that is vulnerable.

The fact that deer are animals of prey suggests looking at where we are vulnerable as well. Where do we allow people to devour us, take advantage of us, use us, disrespect our beliefs and boundaries? Why do we think we deserve this treatment? This is another opportunity to look at the beliefs we were taught about ourselves. Was Carol called stupid as a child? Was she berated for not doing things correctly? Carol had a belief instilled in her at a very young age that she was unimportant and not worthy of affection, generosity, and love. Carol grew up with a sister who was considered the golden child.

She could do no wrong in the eyes of her parents and at times Carol felt that she deserved less than her sister. Why would she believe otherwise when that is what she was taught as a young child? Her father favored the sister even more than the mother did, which would explain Carol's choice in a man who treated her as unimportant. She needed to understand that her belief that she was unworthy and unlovable was based on lies she accepted from very fallible authorities. It's unfortunate that we allow other people to determine our value, but we do it at an unconscious level. Don't blame yourself for your personal beliefs about yourself. Do try to recognize and see them for what they are, lies. Claim your power and determine your own value. You are priceless.

We also need to take responsibility for this part of us. The part of us that believes we deserve to be treated badly, used, or abused. Carol needed to take responsibility for choosing to be with someone who bullied her, degraded her, and took advantage of her generosity. She needed to take back her power and realize her inherent self-worth.

It's a good idea to look at the predators of the animal and see what part of the predator we can call on to protect us from predation. Carol's boyfriend had many of the attributes of the cat. The mountain lion is a predominant predator of deer. Do you remember the symbolism of the house cat? The wild cat is very similar. Cats do what they want when they want. There is a negative side to this. While cats set personal boundaries, they do not respect the personal boundaries of others. Cats don't care about the needs or opinions of others. They are rather hedonistic, interested only in their own pleasure. Carol's boyfriend was not generous, he often refused to contribute financially to their household. He took advantage of her and didn't recognize her boundaries but set very strong boundaries for himself.

Carol needed to be more like the cat and set healthy boundaries for herself. This can only happen when she realizes her self-worth and that she deserves respect. It does no good to figure out the symbolism of an issue if we don't take steps to change the beliefs and behaviors we have that contribute to self-defeating patterns. Someone with a strong sense of self-worth doesn't allow themselves to be treated as a useful object. Healthy people don't attract unhealthy people. Get healthy. If we want a fulfilling relationship with equity and love, we need to know that we are worthy of it.

When counseling people who have erroneous perceptions that they are unimportant and unlovable due to their early childhood experiences I will often ask them to consider how they would feel if they had been put up for adoption as a baby.

Imagine that you were adopted by a loving couple that adored you. You were their only child and they showered you with love and affection. What a cherished baby and child you were. As you grew they respected your boundaries and let you pursue your dreams. They respected your opinion and allowed you to make mistakes and learn without judgment. You were taught that you were important and valuable. You were raised by healthy people. This doesn't mean that the adopted "you" deserves more than the "you" who was raised by your parents. If your parents didn't realize how precious you are it doesn't mean that you aren't precious.

It means you were raised by flawed parents who didn't recognize your magnificence. All parents are flawed. We all do the best we can at any given time. Remember we are all equally lovable and cherished as Children of God.

Don't let the circumstances of your birth define your self-worth! Don't let wounded people form your identity. You are not who you were conditioned to believe you are. You are an integral part of the universe.

The routes to New Jersey for Carol and her boyfriend were very different indeed. Her boyfriend's route went by smokestacks, refineries, inner city slums (when he got lost), and factories. What do these different landscapes represent to you?

All of the symbolism of their different journeys showed Carol that the relationship didn't serve her at all and that she needed to explore why she would put herself in that situation, especially since it wasn't the first relationship she had in which she was treated without regard for her needs, desires, and feelings. Due to Carol's issues with self-worth, she had a long-standing pattern of attraction to men who didn't value her. It was the beginning of great changes in Carol and how she perceived herself and her place in the universe.

Carol recognized some of her responsibility for the relationship, too. Her need to be loved placed a significant burden on her boyfriend. He was incapable due to his own wounds of giving love and affection, he felt too vulnerable to open himself up to someone. Carol needed a lot of reinforcement to believe she was loved because of her childhood. It was a burden he couldn't fulfill. Realize how worthy you are and don't expect a wounded partner to supply you with the love and healing that you deserve.

If Carol had continued in that relationship she wouldn't have been as likely to experience a connection to her Grace. She started to listen to her intuition. She had told her boyfriend that if she had been given the right directions they wouldn't be where they were. Carol started following the right direction, her perfect intuition, and she is in a much better place.

CHAPTER 20

Kangaroo in Space

Last night I was thinking about dreams and how bizarre they can be. Can we really interpret anything? What instantly came into my mind was a vision of me in a small pod-like spaceship. A kangaroo was piloting the rocket and I was in the co-pilot seat. He kept saying to me, "No worries, Mate, everything is under control." Seriously, that's what popped into my head!

How do you interpret something like that? I was baffled. Then I simply began to ask questions. Whenever a symbol isn't obvious, ask questions.

What is a kangaroo? I remembered that just a few days before I had read about opossums, the only marsupial in North America. This is a synchronicity. The information I read was that all marsupials, like the kangaroo, give birth to their offspring prematurely. The babies are birthed into a pouch that has teats that the immature baby suckles on and slowly it becomes viable. If the baby were to be removed from the pouch too soon it would die.

I then asked what birth means. There is nothing more creative than birth. Any symbolism around birth and new life is more than likely about creativity. What creative pursuit am I involved with now? This book is a creation. It is my baby. Like the baby kangaroo, if I bring the book forward too quickly it won't be viable. It needs to be nurtured. I need to make sure the book provides significant information. It needs to be easily understood and written in an engaging style. It must have a positive message, one that feels true to me and to the reader. It must be organized and focused. I must write it when I am in high vibration so that the reader is lifted as they read. Above all it must serve the Highest Good. Everything must be prepared and made ready for its birth. This message informs me that if I bring this book forward before I have fully nurtured it along it will not be viable.

On the emotional and Spiritual levels, I believe this is telling me that growing is a process. We can't grow beyond a spiritual level that we are not physically, emotionally, or vibrationally ready for. When we reach a new level of growth we must acclimate.

If you climbed Mount Everest, you would find the path to the summit is strewn with discarded gear. For us to proceed to the next emotional or spiritual level we must leave behind more of our past negative constructs, the useless baggage that only weighs us down. Our belief that we are not good enough, not worthy, is probably the most universal negative self-belief and one of the most harmful.

As you get closer to the summit of Mount Everest you will find that there is less debris. Because we leave behind our negative self-beliefs as we climb our emotional/spiritual mountain we find that we are becoming acclimated to a life of abundance and joy, a life of Truth.

We begin to accept our worth. We even begin to experience happiness. True happiness that isn't transient or dependent on anything external. There may still be a few beliefs that are weighing us down, but they are discarded more readily and with greater ease as our frequency rises. We become finely adept at recognizing our negative emotional responses and seeing them for what they are, erroneous indoctrinated beliefs that we happily drop.

The most important belief to discard is that we are separate from Source Energy and each other. We are no more separate than the air is from the sky.

At the summit of our Mount Everest, we will not find a flag that signifies we have reached our goal. We will know we have reached it because we are at Peace and in Truth. We can see everything clearly from the top of the world. When everything is crumbling around us we have a center of Grace and Love. We have let go of all that held us back. We are aware that we are part of the One Consciousness.

To move on we must have faith in Divine Order. Divine Order may not match our desired or expected timeline. That tiny kangaroo baby may want to bounce out of the pouch but can't because the time is not right. When we are ready the next step will be shown to us. Have faith in your progress and know that you are exactly where you need to be.

The space ship? If I do have patience and get the work done and allow it to grow into its fullness then it will rocket out of this universe, it will "take off." In the story of the kangaroo and me I feel like I'm heading into uncharted territory. The kangaroo is assuring me that all will be well, that everything is under control, even when

I'm fearful that I'm on a fool's errand. When a rocket leaves earth it almost immediately discards it boosters. As it heads into orbit there are parts of the rocket no longer needed. The same is true for us.

Space also represents absence. It is a place that has no gravity. It doesn't pull us down to earth. The sky has always represented heaven to people. Earth often represents ego. If I let go of all my useless constructs, if I use my time to learn and grow, I will come to a place of spaciousness. A place devoid of unnecessary thought and limiting beliefs.

Have faith that there is Divine Order and though we may not see it, it is working in our best interest. Know that we can't rush creation. The me in the co-pilot seat is anxious, that is ego me, worried my work will be fruitless and fail. The Kangaroo, my Higher Self, the real pilot, wants me to know that everything is under control, not the ego's control, but Divine Order. My Higher Self is writing this book, not my ego. Going where no one has gone before can be scary to the ego. My Kangaroo Higher Self reminds me that all is well. With faith we can go from Down Under to Outer Space. No worries, Mate.

What do you do if you ask for the meaning of the symbolism presented to you and you don't get an immediate response? You wait, you have faith. It will come in Divine Order. The beauty of recognizing and interpreting the symbolism in our life is that we can use it to consciously inform our decisions. It gives us direction. It highlights our strengths and weaknesses. It reveals subconscious beliefs so that we can start to change our inner dialogue. Symbols stop us from continuing patterns that aren't working for us. Symbolism is a guidance system for our personal rocket ship.

If you trust the symbolism in your life, it can save you a lot of time and suffering. If you dismiss a symbol and just go forward without heeding its message then another symbol will come to you, the next one stronger and more insistent. Your Divine Knowing, in sending these messages to you, wants you to fulfill yourself as soon as possible and if you don't respond it will get louder and louder and sometimes it will put you in some difficult circumstances to get its point across. Listen to the nudges before you get to a point of suffering. We'd all prefer the tap on the shoulder to the hammer on the head.

Try this exercise. Tell your imagination to present you with a picture, a brief story, and then analyze the symbolism of it. What does your Higher Self want you to know?

CHAPTER 21

Warts and All

As my friend, Anna, and I hiked along a path through the woods she saw no less than seven toads. She spotted every one of them before me. That's a lot of toads. I don't usually see seven toads during the whole season.

What was Toad trying to tell her? Let's look at Toad's life. Toads are lovely, some think they're ugly, little amphibians. Like frogs they are born in the water from a gelatinous egg sac as tadpoles, which then morph into toads. Unlike frogs, toads spend their life on land except when breeding. It sheds its skin as frog does. Toads are quirky little creatures. They sit very calmly and are usually very well hidden in their homes in the woods or garden. Seeing seven toads is highly unusual. Synchronicities like this are telling us to listen to their message.

As we were walking through the woods, before we saw our first toad, Anna told me that she felt she was about to go through some big changes. She felt that an important time of transformation was about to begin. Toad validated that statement. Toad, like Frog, is about transformation.

The fact that Toad only returns to water (Source Energy) when it is mating and laying eggs (creating) represents the fact we are at our best when we are inspired to create. When we are immersed in a project we are passionate about we are channeling our Highest Self. There is nothing that feels better than inspired work.

Toad is well camouflaged, blending in beautifully. If I was Anna, I would ask if I was afraid to let others see me? Do we tend to hide in the crowd because we feel inferior and unworthy of recognition, do we fade into the background so others don't see all our imagined faults and failings, or because we don't think anyone could possibly love us as we are? Do we present a role in public, the mask of normalcy because we feel too vulnerable to be authentic, we are afraid we will be judged as harshly as we judge ourselves? Because toads are so well camouflaged and Anna saw seven of them, I think toad was telling her to come out from hiding. Be proud, be seen.

Whether you want to blend in or are happier as the center of attention doesn't matter if it comes from a place of authenticity. You may be the quiet one because you have no need to be accepted, no need to be heard; your soul speaks on a level beyond words and actions. You have no need to have your ego accepted by other egos. It is when your behavior is a need, a plead, a way of saying, "please accept me and love me, please notice me, approve of me, let me know I matter, validate that I am normal and fit in," that it is coming from ego, from fear.

Toad wants you to accept yourself as you are. They want you to love yourself, warts and all. You may have heard the old tales that toads give you warts. Those stories come from their bumpy skin. They look like they have warts. The thing is Toad loves herself very much. She doesn't care what others think of her. She doesn't have to present herself as anything but what she is. She doesn't feel a need to explain herself or make excuses. She knows she is an embodiment of the Divine just as she is. She sits in calm, peaceful acceptance of who she is. Toads are just happy to be. They sit humbly and proudly. Buddha Toad.

This is an area in which my friend has struggled. Growing up she heard from her mother that she was lucky to have her looks because she didn't have anything else going for her. She had trouble with the teaching techniques of her childhood schools, which reinforced her belief that all she had was her beauty. When she was young she believed it would probably be best if she died before her looks went. Growing old without her physical attractiveness scared her.

One of her destructive thinking patterns when she was younger and thought about attempting something new or "big" was, "Who do you think you are? Why would you think you could do that?" This was a learned mantra. The low opinion of herself she was taught as a child stayed with her, as our own childhood beliefs stay with us until we bring them to light.

Toad brought such beautiful validation to my friend's work on self-love. After our walk we did a visualization made specifically to help her with these issues of self-worth. If you have beliefs that you don't contribute anything special to the world, that you don't make a difference, you may want to try this visualization.

Before you start ask yourself what some of your conditioned limiting beliefs are. Do you feel you're not as important as others? Do you feel like others don't see you, you're invisible? Do you feel unworthy of love? Do you suffer from lack of abundance and think it will never come to you? Do you think you will never find your true passion or purpose? Do you think you are stupid? Do you think you are homely? Do you think you will always be unhealthy? Do you believe yourself to be less than others? Do you believe you can never be loved? Do you believe you can never be forgiven?

Like many of my visualization tools it starts with imagining yourself walking alongside a river. On your right you see your childhood home, your first school, and your first church. Include any other buildings that significantly influenced your early years, perhaps a grandparent's or friend's home. You notice them, but you don't need to bring up any memories. If memories appear just let them float by. You can explore them if they are persistent.

Up ahead on the left you see a bridge across the river. When you reach it, you walk across. On the other side is a path through the woods. You start walking down the path. You may or may not see anyone on this path. If you do, it may be a person you know, perhaps one who has passed on, it may be an animal, or it may be someone you don't know. It may be an angel, faery, troll, or guide. If you do meet someone and you'd like to talk, take a few moments to stop and listen, to say and hear what you need. Continue your path when you are ready. You will come to a clearing. The sun is setting. In the clearing is a bonfire. Surrounding the bonfire are many people and, possibly, other beings. Some you will know, some you may not.

As you start to walk around the circle of beings you notice that each one holds a piece of paper, written upon each one is an old limiting belief you have about yourself. You read each one and then throw it into the flames. If you can't read it, don't worry, just throw it in the fire knowing it is a lie about yourself that you have believed. You are transforming it into the Divine Energy it was before it was denied by the collective and turned into a lie.

When you have thrown all the lies into the fire, you see a large gift bag. Pick it up. Go around the fire again. You will give each being a gift from the bag. Each gift represents a beautiful, unique, and exquisite part of who you are. You may give them a jewel, a pinecone, a toy boat, a bird's nest, a seashell, a can opener, a cup of water, a leaf, a radio, a book, a magical silver amulet. Whatever you pull out of your bag you give them. They are all so happy to receive these amazing gifts from you. You all share a moment of joy together. They feel grateful for the gifts you bring to the world; the gifts are unique to you alone. You are very necessary here. Without you the universe would be incomplete. Everyone around the fire realizes this and knows how important you and your gifts are. Some of them may apologize for not recognizing your importance or your gifts earlier. It is then you realize you knew of your special gifts all along. You don't need their approval or their acceptance, but you appreciate their kind words.

Next you see a table with a beautiful crystal pitcher filled with clear water, and fluted glasses. You fill each glass and give one to each being. You all take a drink of this refreshing, exhilarating water. There is now a lightness of being and a heady feeling of unlimited potential that permeates the gathering and fills you. You and all the beings begin to dance around the bonfire. The sparks fly into the beautiful night sky. It is a celebration of who you truly are.

Do this visualization before you read on.

After the meditation you may want to review the gifts that you remember giving. What do they symbolize? A pinecone might symbolize your unlimited potential. The pinecone also represents the pineal gland, which is shaped like a pinecone and many believe to be the seat of the soul in our body. Seeds grow into mighty trees. A seashell may represent the ocean, symbolizing the Divine in you or the being you gave it to. A bowl of food may represent abundance or nurturing. A radio might represent your frequency, how you express the Divine. If you don't immediately recognize the symbolism, simply enjoy the feeling of the gift. These gifts you gave to others are also gifts to yourself. What does sharing water symbolize to you? How do you feel when you dance? Does anyone or anything stand out in this visualization? Why? How did you feel after you gave the gifts? Did any of the beings speak to you?

Toad's message is so beautiful. I love myself warts and all. Not one of us is perfect on this earth. Yet, we all expect ourselves to live up to standards of perfection that prevent us from fully loving ourselves. So what, you're not the best looking person in the world, not the smartest, not the youngest or oldest, not the best dancer, singer, cook, mechanic, doctor, actor, child, artist, parent, or person. Give yourself a break! Accept yourself. Are you as hard on anyone else as you are on yourself?

Probably not. Would you talk to a friend the way you talk to yourself or allow a friend to speak to you like that? Never! You often forgive others more easily than you forgive yourself. Give yourself the compassion that you give others. There is no one, absolutely no one else that is you. You are so very important in bringing the world and all its people to the Divine Vibration we will reach. You are unique and it can't be done without you. Right now, start seeing yourself as Toad sees you, you really are the perfect you, just as you are, warts and all.

CHAPTER 22

The Coin of Heaven

Sarah had a recurring dream for as long as she could remember. In the dream she is about 11 years old. The setting of the dream is Israel. What does Israel represent? Israel is the Promised Land in the Bible. It is called the Land of Milk and Honey for its abundant pasture and farmland. It is a symbol of plenty.

In the dream she is at a country club setting (more abundance imagery) by the swimming pool. The swimming pool, water, would represent God. No one was there that she knew, but she didn't feel alone. There were mostly women about sixty years old in one-piece black bathing suits and flowered bathing caps, 1960's attire, the time of the original dream. They were lounging and chatting comfortably.

Younger men, women, and children were in the pool diving to retrieve ancient silver and gold coins from the bottom of the pool. When they surfaced they would come up to the side of the pool and put their coins into individual piles. Some piles of coins were neatly stacked, some were just heaps, and others were placed in containers made specifically for the coins.

Clearly, one thing coins represent is abundance. After diving to retrieve coins, Sara put her coins in a container made just for them. This would indicate that Sarah was taught that money is special. She surfaced to find her coins were gone. She asked everyone why someone would steal her coins when it was so easy to get them.

Sarah started having this dream as a child. She was conditioned to believe that she can't trust others with her money. This theme of money grabbing and greed was rife in her birth family. The ones stealing the coins in her dream represent the part of her that believes her birth family programming.

While writing this chapter, a phrase, the coin of heaven, popped into my head. This is what intuition looks like, seemingly random thoughts that grab your attention. I did an internet search. In the 1950's, Neville Goddard was one of the first practitioners and teachers of what is popularly known as The Law of Attraction. *The Coin of Heaven* was a lecture series, which he compiled into a book. He taught that we create our reality from our imagination and that what we desire is already available to us and waiting for us to accept it. He believed that if we ask, it is given. In her dream a part of Sarah, her unconditioned psyche, knew that abundance is easy; she asked why anyone would steal the coins acquired with such ease. She was clearly questioning the programming of her family and culture.

The older women represent the Crone, the wise woman. They wore flowered bathing caps. Since they are on the crown chakra, they represent the blossoming of our Divine Self. The crown chakra is the place on our body where Source Energy enters us. They are basking in the sun, the masculine symbol of God which balances their Divine Feminine symbolism. They are happy with what they have and don't need stacks of money to prove they are worthy. They occasionally get up and take a swim and then go back to their lounge chairs. They know they are fully loved and are content in that knowing. They relax with Source Energy. After all, they are in the land of milk and honey, the promised land. They signify what Sarah's Higher Self, the Wise Woman, Intuition, wants her to claim, her inherent worthiness and abundance. Abundance is easy.

We attract at the level of our frequency. Our frequency is determined by our beliefs, emotions, and thoughts. What is your definition of abundance? For some it's being grateful for what they have. When we put out the vibration of gratitude, we receive more to be thankful for. Gratitude is the easiest path to abundance. The people diving to retrieve coins were getting their money easily through Vibration/Spirit/ God/ Energy, symbolized by the water. Abundance, like any other creation, is energetic. Her family said don't trust anyone, there isn't enough money for us all. Her Higher Self in the dream tells her that getting money is easy.

On a spiritual level the dream is saying that God is where you will find true abundance. It is saying we only crave material abundance because of our programming, it will not bring us lasting happiness. Sara was upset after finding that her coins had been stolen. *Anything that can cause unhappiness by its loss will never bring us lasting happiness because while in ego mind we will always fear its loss.* Reclaiming our connection to God, to Oneness, will bring us lasting joy and peace.

Let's look at the ego lie from a societal viewpoint. We can live the "American" dream if we work hard. So, to live in abundance according to this collective paradigm we must work hard. Wait a minute. Aren't there some very rich people who have never worked hard? And people who work like dogs, with two or more jobs just to survive? Haven't some people been "lucky?" The belief that abundance will always come if we work hard is not true. A true universal law works in all instances.

The dream was a gift to her, but she didn't understand it. It became a recurring dream because she wasn't comprehending its message.

Sarah still struggles in her life with emotions and paradigms concerning money. She thinks her family is robbing her of her inheritance and they may very well be as they were all raised to think you need to take from others to have for yourself. She thinks she needs to work at a job she hates to get money. The dream is telling her if she just believes God's promise of the reward of milk and honey in the promised land she will be in abundance. Stop striving and start thriving!

At the end of the dream, Sarah looked across the desert sand and saw mountains in the distance. Suddenly, as dreams happen, Sarah is running across the desert, chased by people with archaic weapons. She jumps into the air, turns into a flying cat, and flies away from them, laughing, towards the mountain. End of Dream.

The desert would represent barrenness, a complete lack of abundance. She is running away from people who want to harm her. The people chasing represent the people who told her the lies about lack as well as the part of her that believes them. The archaic weapons represent the lies themselves, of not enough, of greed and money grabbing as a necessity. One of the synonyms of archaic is obsolete. These paradigms of life that tell us to do what we hate to survive, that we can't trust anyone, that we need to step on others to get abundance are outdated and useless tools. They lead to a barren life without joy, love, or connection. This erroneous belief system is the only thing that is hurting her chance for happiness and abundance. As a society we are waking up to the fact that connection, creativity, love, and leisure are more important than stuff.

She turns into a flying cat. Remember cats, they do what they want. Sarah needs to stop trying to fit in, stop looking for approval, stop working at a job she hates, stop believing in limitation, start trusting, and start doing what fills her with happiness and passion, only then will more of the same come her way. She needs to set boundaries with her family, the way cats set boundaries. She needs to claim self-authority and stop kowtowing to her programming.

In the dream she decides she's had enough of the ego's attacks and lies. She starts to do what she wants (cat), running from the lies (archaic weapons), and flies away (rising above earthly limiting beliefs), to the mountain (the highest point we can go, the Higher Self). She is laughing because she experiences the joy of freedom. Freedom comes with consciousness. When she was in the altered dream state while asleep, she became conscious that her beliefs are useless lies.

There is another symbol to explore and that is the "ancient" coins of gold and silver. Gold and silver are considered the two most valuable metals in the world.

Silver is often associated with the moon, the Divine Feminine while gold is associated with the sun, the Divine Masculine. These coins were in water (Source Energy). They represent the most valuable coin we can acquire, Wisdom, Truth, Knowing, Love, Peace. Whatever you want to call it. The Perfect Balance. The Coin of Heaven. At its highest level this dream is telling Sara to let go of the need for earthly treasure and seek the Highest Truth, only Love is real. Peace comes from the knowing of this Truth.

Constantly worrying about money is no way to live. Sarah won't understand the highest meaning of the Coin of Heaven until she accepts that she has been taught false paradigms based in fear of lack, perhaps the biggest fear faced in materialistic societies.

The concepts of competition and lack were created by society. It is a collective belief to which we have all agreed. The fear of lack, the consciousness of victimhood, has been the prevailing paradigm since before the days of lords and serfs. As individuals we can agree to new empowering beliefs. We can accept the personal power we possess through our Higher Self and lift the collective to the Truth; we can have and deserve abundance. We are not victims; we are powerful beings of unlimited potential worthy of a fulfilling life.

Remember who you are. You are a Divine Creation of Love worthy of abundance. Nothing external determines your abundance. *You are the creator of your life.*

CHAPTER 23

Out on a Limb

As my marriage was deteriorating I had three dreams in quick succession. Two of the dreams I had in one night.

In the first dream our next-door neighbor was in our front yard tilling a small patch of soil. He kept tilling and sowing seeds, but nothing grew. He was working on the same area over and over and nothing grew. The land was obviously barren and yet he kept trying to get something to grow. He wouldn't give up.

That same night I dreamt I was vacuuming our living room carpet. I kept going over and over it with the vacuum, but it wouldn't come clean. It wasn't getting rid of any of the dirt. It was a waste of effort, but in the dream, I just couldn't accept that and kept trying to get it clean.

My husband and I were in counseling at the time. I knew the dreams were related to our marriage and our efforts to save it.

In the first dream my next-door neighbor symbolized a part of me. What did I think of my next-door neighbor? How would I briefly describe him? I immediately thought that he was a very intelligent man, which begs the question, why would he continue to do something over and over that didn't yield any progress or results. He was in our front yard representing the future, which meant the future of our marriage held no promise of any kind. It was a barren wasteland. Our continued marriage counseling would be fruitless.

In the second dream I was doing a similar thing, doing something over and over that wasn't helping. This was in the house, which symbolizes the present. I was being told the counseling, all the work I was doing wasn't producing results. Nothing was being "cleaned up" through the counseling.

In the third dream we lived in a big, old Victorian house. It was the kind of house that you might look at and think of family and tradition, of happier times; times when kids chased fireflies in the yard at twilight and Mom and Dad sat on the front porch relaxing at the end of the day. It was a house that represented to me the ideal family. But the house was in terrible disrepair, practically falling down.

I climbed an enormous oak tree close to the house hoping to fix it. I climbed up high into the tree and out onto the end of a branch to try and repair the old falling down house. Then someone that I didn't know was on the ground yelling up to me to come down. She was telling me that I couldn't fix it, to give up, that it was too much of a risk. She warned me I would fall if I kept trying. She told me the house was beyond repair. Get out of that tree! End of Dream.

I knew the house represented our marriage. It was a mess. I was doing everything I could to make it work because my marriage and family represented so much to me. This was the role we were raised to play, the marriage and family we were promised would be happily ever after. I was "going out on a limb" in my desire to make it work, but it just couldn't be saved. The person standing on the ground and yelling up to me was the part of me that "I didn't know." It was my intuition. I wasn't in touch with the part of me that knew the truth. The marriage was over, and I needed to accept that. If I continued this course of action, trying to revive a marriage beyond repair, it would only lead to more pain.

These dreams were very clear in their message, but it still took me a long time to give up on the marriage. I now try to listen to the signs, symbols, and synchronicities that I receive and accept the truth in them, and most importantly, act on their message when I know in my heart it is true. We do ourselves a terrible disservice and waste precious time when we live in denial and refuse to take heed of our intuitive messages.

Is there a part of you that you don't know? Are there parts of you that are on autopilot, patterns that you repeat without conscious examination? We all have our learned behaviors; we all have habitual responses. Consciousness needs practice. Practice brings increases in our happiness quotient. Is there anything more important?

CHAPTER 24

Snapping Turtle

D enise took a trip to visit her parents in Florida. As she was driving towards an intersection early one morning she saw that the car ahead of her was stopped and blocking traffic in her lane. Denise moved into the next lane. As she drove by she saw a woman trying to protect a snapping turtle crossing the road. Denise pulled around the corner and parked her car. She walked over to help the woman and the turtle.

The turtle had kept moving so the woman had turned her car on the diagonal and was blocking the whole side of the road. A man in a car behind her had also gotten out to help. At this point the turtle was in the middle of the intersection.

The three of them worked to get the turtle across the road in the direction it was moving. It's not easy to move a snapping turtle. The snapper was getting very agitated as the man tried to pick it up. The turtle's shell was also very slippery making it hard for the man to grip it. Denise went to her car and retrieved a black shawl to place over the turtle. The shawl calmed the turtle. It blocked out the world and gave the man some purchase on the shell. They were able to get the turtle across the intersection into a dry canal that led to a pond. They couldn't get it all the way to the water, but they got it to safety and closer to its destination.

The first thing that popped into my mind was that a block had been placed in front of Denise. At first, she didn't know why, so she started to move along in another lane. Then she saw the reason for the block. Sometimes in our lives we experience obstacles to our goals. We often try to push through or go around without questioning why we are being blocked. The Universe is trying to tell her in this symbolism to investigate what is preventing her from enjoying a better life.

Turtles have a hard shell. What could this mean? Does Denise have a hard shell? Has she built up walls? Does she keep people out? Does she believe she needs to protect herself from a cruel world? Is she afraid to come out of her shell? Is she always guarded when she's with other people? What would you ask?

What are the questions for the opposite aspect of shells? Does Denise let people take advantage of her? Does she need to develop a harder shell? Does she have clear boundaries for how she allows people to treat her? Does she need to protect herself more from outside influence?

This was a Florida Snapping turtle. I learned they are different from northern snappers as they develop hard spikes on the outside of their shells. Each year the spikes grow a little longer and larger to further protect the turtle. This would tell me that Denise developed her protective exterior over time. She may not have felt safe or protected as a child. This could have been with her family, at school, or with peers. Considering that this symbolic event occurred while visiting her parents suggests it was a familial wound that caused her to build her emotional armor.

In water snapping turtles feel safe. It's their element. Water signifies the One Consciousness. However, when Snappers are out of their element, on land (representing the Ego) they feel vulnerable and tend to be more reactive, striking out before they establish whether something is a threat. Does Denise tend to be defensive, making assumptions and snapping at people without first getting all the necessary information? Does she do the opposite by allowing resentments and anger to build up until she snaps and lashes out? Just think of the word snap when used to describe human behavior. He snapped at his little boy when he spilled his milk. She snapped at her employee for making the mistake. When the car in front of her turned without signaling she snapped and went into full road rage.

Helping children develop conscious and thoughtful responses when young prevents reactive behavior in adulthood. Discussing a situation before it becomes an issue, getting all the information, allowing someone to respond before making assumptions are healthy ways to deal with our perceptions. It is better to clarify before you need to apologize.

Did Denise feel attacked as a child? Was she allowed to defend herself if her parents thought she did something wrong? If her parents were reactive, it may be why she developed a hard shell and attacked others without reasonable cause.

This symbolism tells Denise (the turtle) that when she is in Truth and Love (the water), she feels safe and doesn't feel the need to attack. When we are in alignment with the One Consciousness we are in our true power. We don't take anything personally, we don't feel threatened by the behavior of others, we don't need to blame. We understand that people are acting from a place of wounded ego *that has nothing to do with us.*

It's almost impossible for us mere humans to be constantly in a state of Divine Truth, of knowing that we are all One. When Denise forgets who she is and believes she is a separate person (on land, in the ego) she lives on edge, in fear of attack, as we all do to different degrees.

Denise tends to overreact and finds herself in difficult situations because of her inappropriate responses. Her reactions are stronger than what a situation calls for or they are completely unfounded. She knows she has this problem, and it has interfered in her professional life to the point where she received a warning for her verbal attack on a fellow employee. She later found out that she had made a wrong assumption. Her personal relationships suffer because of her reactionary behavior as well.

When on dry land, in Ego, Denise needs help. She can't get herself (the turtle/ego) to Consciousness (water) alone. She needs to balance the feminine side of herself, which is being open, listening, and waiting patiently and the masculine side of herself which is action. The feminine side (the other woman who stopped her car) doesn't try to move the turtle alone. She waits for help. This means that Denise needs to ask for help when she finds herself emotionally reactive, when she's reacting in

Ego and feels like she's going to "snap." The man (masculine) tries to move the turtle forward, but the turtle is agitated at this point (in ego). The people were trying to help the turtle, but the turtle erroneously thought they were attacking it. Denise (more feminine) puts a shawl over it and the turtle calms.

The shawl would be a message to Denise that if she is feeling overwhelmed or attacked that she can pull a veil over the Ego until she calms down. Taking a few deep breaths may allow her to calm down. It may be time to close her eyes, sit in stillness, and wait for the peace of God to come. She could leave the room for a few moments to release the heightened emotion. At that point of peace (after the turtle calms from being under the shawl) the masculine picks up the turtle and brings it to a place where it has a much better chance of getting to God (symbolized by the pond, water). Very simply this message is telling Denise to pause and calm herself before reacting to any encounter that brings up an emotional disturbance in her. She needs to remain passive, the feminine, and evaluate the situation and her response calmly, without assuming, before taking any action, the masculine.

This all points to being slow and deliberate in our responses to situations that illicit defensiveness. Turtles are universally thought of as slow animals. Taking a long time to reach a destination is a symbol of the turtle. When we rush and act without thinking we may end up wasting time and reaching an outcome that we don't desire.

Denise may want to start asking questions when she feels her emotions rise. She can examine her thoughts and ask if they are true or if she is assuming. She can ask the person to whom she is reacting questions to clarify her perception before responding. She may work on realizing that it's pointless to take things personally. Even if the person is attacking her, they are doing it from a place of ego and it doesn't relate to her at all. She may represent a familial figure to them, and their ego is being triggered by a past incident unrelated to her. Or they may represent a familial figure to her and trigger her feelings of defensiveness.

We can't overlook the intersection in this symbolic event. Denise was at an intersection in her life. Whether it was career, relationship, or spiritual in nature doesn't really matter. She was symbolically stuck in the middle of the road with little hope of getting across without getting crushed by a car. She needed help navigating this transition. Denise was trying to make decisions based in ego (while on dry land). Her reactionary conditioning was interfering with her chances of success. She can't get to Truth until she stops her reactionary, ego driven behavior and listens to her intuition, her Higher Self.

While in ego we make decisions based in fear. In ego we want the fastest reward and often that reward is the comfortable and known familiar, old patterns of living, whether they work or not. If we want to change and move forward, we can't regress to the familiar. It's another attempt by the ego at self-sabotage.

Our emotions are a gift telling us to stop and look at what is disturbing our peace. It is not what is happening that disturbs our peace, it is our reaction to it. We need to take some time to calm ourselves and objectively examine the situation and our reaction. What is the root cause of our reaction to this type of situation? Where is it familiar?

The turtle, when under the shawl, was in a place of quiet and stillness. Only then are we able to move forward with right action. Take some deep, calming breaths. Close your eyes and meditate. When you ask for guidance and give up control you put the question into the best hands, the hands of your Higher Self. We can't hear the One Consciousness when we're feeling attacked, our default is to snap. Trust that the answer will be given. When we get an answer from our place of peace, we can act.

CHAPTER 25

It's a Wonderful Day in the Neighborhood

I woke up this morning with the last bit of a dream in my head. In the dream my youngest daughter and I were trying to do something, to achieve some goal. I'm not sure what, but we were not meeting with success. We decided to close our eyes and sit quietly in joy for a few minutes to see if that would bring us results. We opened our eyes, looked at each other, and stuck out our tongues to see if we had succeeded. On each of our tongues was a beautifully cut aquamarine in a silver lining. We were so excited that we did it right and got these jewels on our tongues. When I awoke I felt really happy.

What does this dream mean? To put it in context I had visited my daughter the evening before and she was complaining of having had a bad day, being anxious, and feeling unproductive. I told her that I was great at giving advice but not so good at just listening and keeping my mouth shut. We laughed and I kept my mouth shut.

We decided to have a quiet evening and watched a documentary about Fred Rogers of the PBS show, Mr.

Roger's Neighborhood. It was so sweet, and we were both moved to tears by the beautiful work of Mr. Rogers and his genuine loving heart.

What does the dream mean? Does it have anything to do with Mr. Rogers? Does it have anything to do with me keeping my mouth shut? Let's deconstruct it.

In the dream we were trying to see what worked and what results we would get. We hadn't been successful with anything we tried. Our actions were not producing our desired outcome. We decided to sit quietly in joy. We closed our eyes and sat in silence. This makes me think of meditation. In meditation we close our eyes and sit in stillness. We are becoming silent so that we can hear God.

Then we opened our mouths and we had jewels on our tongues. Not just any jewels, but aquamarines. What is the origin of the word aquamarine? Aqua means water and marine means sea. We are back to the ocean, water, the symbol of God, the Creative Source from which all else arises. We had God, or Love, on our tongues.

What does the tongue and mouth represent? Talking is about communication and expressing ourselves. We enjoy food. Food nurtures our body. What nurtures our soul? To me the aquamarine on our tongues symbolizes the expression of God. God doesn't express in words, but in vibration, in frequency. It represents the nurturing quality of God's Love and how expressing God's Love nurtures others. We can accomplish so much more expressing God through vibration than with any words.

One thing we learned from the documentary on Mr. Rogers was that he went to seminary and was an ordained minister. He would symbolize a Man of God.

He expressed himself through the medium of TV. TV is sent to us in frequency. He communicated Love (God) to all who watched and listened to him. He expressed the Divine as not many people do on this plane, in a quiet and humble way. His ingenuous nature and pure love of people allowed us to believe him when he told us we are loved just the way we are. Do you love yourself just the way you are?

The aquamarine on our tongues signifies that we can express God to the world without words. We aren't being called to preach or even to speak. When our vibration is in sync with the frequency of our Higher Being our energy and essence is one of Love. This energy affects the energy of those around us. When we express Love by being present in the vibration of God, we raise the vibration of the people with us whether we are on the subway, shopping, walking down the street, or with friends and family. When we really think about it, vibrating at the frequency of Love is so much more helpful to people than talking to them. Words can't convey the Divine. Language is insufficient to express God. Nothing heals or helps more than Divine Presence. If you have someone that you can't talk with about their behaviors or their unhappiness, you can still be the presence of Divine Love when you are with them. We eventually reach a point where we don't need to think about expressing Love, we become Love and that vibration is always expressing through us.

The aquamarine on our tongues would also suggest that when we are aligned with God our words will be inspired by Divine Love. When we are intuitively called to speak we can be sure the words will be right. We will be able to nurture others with our frequency as well as inspired words.

The aquamarine had a silver lining. The silver lining in this story is that if we are present in our Higher Self, expressing Love, we get back what we are giving and will live in joy. What could be a better silver lining than that?

CHAPTER 26

Wash Away the Shame

The bathroom is where we clean ourselves and, as we found out earlier, it's where we get rid of sh*t. Let's look at some bathroom symbolism.

Sink or tub drains clogged? You may have blocks that keep you from letting go of past beliefs. The clogged drain represents the block, the water represents your emotions and your Spiritual Self. Emotions are our first sign of how we are doing on our life path.

Because the main purpose of the sink or tub is for washing, when it's blocked, it may represent feeling dirty in a metaphoric sense. Feeling dirty is a euphemism for shame. Were you made to feel shame as a child? About your behaviors, your intelligence, your body, your gender, your race, religion, your choices?

Since we wash our face and hands at the sink our shame is probably connected to our perception of how the world judges our appearance (face)) or judges what we do (hands). There are many types of shame around the face. Our face may be a clear indicator of our racial or ethnic heritage, of our gender, age, or appearance. Some people are ashamed because they believe they don't fit in. They have been the object of blatant bigotry, they have internalized the social construct of otherness, or their parents were ashamed of their heritage and they accepted the belief. Their face is a daily reminder. It's easy to see how someone can be raised to unconsciously feel shame about their ethnicity, or race.

What if we think we are plain looking or unattractive due to societal and media indicators of beauty? These beliefs are unfortunate, but, again, understandable. The clogged sink suggests that we are inhibiting our life and happiness by holding onto shame over a belief dictated by an external source. Can we consider these issues and make positive steps to correct the beliefs? We are beautiful, no matter what the media or society or any single person tells us. The ideal of beauty changes with the times. True beauty is eternal.

Our hands signify what we do. We may be ashamed of a menial occupation, one that doesn't have the status of white-collar work in our society. Dirty hands (the clogged sink) can also be symbolic of shame for what you have done or what has been done to you in your life. If we are sexually abused, we may have shame around that issue, even though we are not the ones who perpetrated the act. The clogged drain signifies that we are unable to let go of these beliefs that we are dirty and shameful.

Shame is a false construct. Guilt tells us when we have done something considered wrong by us. We can recognize how we missed the mark, learn from it, and move on. Shame, on the other hand, is a form of self-punishment imposed by our programming.

Take stock of where you hold shame and release yourself. See it for what it is, an erroneous emotion that holds us responsible for doing the best we could at any given time in our life. It's the past and it's time to let it go. When we unclog the sink it is symbolic of washing away our shame.

Is the bathtub drain blocked? Since we take baths and showers in the tub this may be about body shame. Are you happy with your glorious body? Body image for women is a major issue in our society and becoming more so for men as well. Look at the constant media representation of the perfect body. Who can live up to those ridiculous standards? We are all so different. We are unique and valuable as we are.

It was very hot the other day and I wondered why I needed to wear clothes. Strange thought, perhaps, but I really questioned it. I thought that if I wanted to go outside in my backyard and do some naked gardening then why shouldn't I be able to without repercussions? If I truly have no shame regarding my body and think the human body is a wonderful, magnificent creation, why not? The answer that popped into my mind was because it would offend someone else's belief about what is appropriate.

We teach our children that we must hide the body. Even mothers breastfeeding in public are denigrated for a beautiful natural act, nurturing their babies. When will we stop perpetuating the construct that the human body is shameful? When will we stop sexualizing the body? The body is such an amazing work of art and function. Let go of shame and embarrassment about your body's size or shape. Let's start to celebrate it as the uniquely beautiful and functional creation that it is.

Is the toilet clogged? Don't hold on to grudges, resentments, jealousies, and hurts. They don't serve you and, in fact, stop you from progressing. Let go of that sh*t. Flush it! Very easy symbolism here, toilet equals poop or pee. Poop and pee represent things we need to get rid of, waste. The only things we need to get rid of are the results of fearful beliefs informed by the collective and internalized. All the past wounds, the resentments, the anger we can't let go of interfere with our lives and block our growth.

Constipation also indicates holding onto resentments, but in that case your personal plumbing is blocked. Any problems releasing waste signify that we haven't yet forgiven a past hurt. Let go of resentments.

Issues with urination are more likely to signify fear or anger. Think of the expressions. She was so pissed off. I was so scared I almost peed my pants. That explains why we can laugh so hard that we pee our pants. Laughter takes us out of ego. We are finally completely letting go. It's the positive aspect of the symbolism. It's fun but can be messy!

Did your toilet overflow? Are you finding yourself in a rage or sobbing uncontrollably because you've been repressing all those resentments and hurts? Are you overwhelmed and unable to control your emotions? Try to do a review and find the source of your emotional trauma and reactivity. It's time to learn to express our emotions as we feel them without thinking that it will hurt us or someone else. It is when we suppress them that we hurt ourselves and others. We can't suppress them forever and so we explode. Like the overflowing toilet, diarrhea is also an indication of suppressed anger that hasn't been addressed and so "explodes."

Sometimes we have bouts of constipation followed by diarrhea. Think about how that makes sense.

Our house has many lessons for us. If we examine issues, like a leaky pipe, or a broken piece of furniture, or a painting falls to the floor, a stove that won't heat up, a refrigerator that stops keeping things cold, a bed that breaks, a door that sticks, and we think about what that area of the house represents and apply it to our lives we can learn a lot about ourselves.

The bedroom is the place where we enter an altered state of consciousness, sleep. Another important aspect of the bedroom if you are in relationship, is that it is the place where you join your sexual/spiritual energy with another, thus making it a sacred space.

Ideally your bedroom should be an environment of calm and relaxation. Green and blue are calming, balancing colors. They are the colors of the ocean, the sky, and the forest so they would denote spirit, eternal love, mystery, and the natural vibration of the soul. Grey, a combination of black and white, would represent balance. Do you have a balanced relationship? If not, this color for your walls or linens may help. If you want more passion in your relationship or more romance go for a color with red undertones, a pink tone.

If you keep an altar, the bedroom is a good place for it. In the bedroom we wake up to begin each new day, having an altar there is a reminder of what is important to us and brings us to mindfulness. A moment of gratitude at our altar each morning sets a meaningful tone for our day. An altar may consist of pictures of your family, it may have representations of Deities, it may be objects from nature, whatever inspires you and makes you feel connected to All. It is symbolic of a commitment to a path of Peace, Love, and Self Awareness.

Try to keep the bedroom simple and clean. A cluttered room represents a cluttered mind, which finds sleep difficult. If the bedroom is a space of order and calm, it will be reflected in your life. It is the room most personal to you. It is a good barometer of where you are and what you need to do to progress.

If dirty clothes are piled up and draped around the room, take stock. Where in your life are you airing your dirty laundry because symbolically it's not being contained? If shoes are scattered around ask yourself if you are stepping forward in life in a random way, allowing life to take you in any direction, or are you making thoughtful decisions and taking deliberate steps.

Do you make your bed every morning? Think of the expression, "you made your bed, now you have to lie in it." If we don't make our bed it would indicate a need to start taking responsibility for our creations.

The kitchen is often called the heart of the home. How is your kitchen? Meals are prepared there. Are they made with nurturing Love? Are they a chore? If you live alone, please give yourself nurturing food. Take time for yourself, prepare it with Love. Use the kitchen to connect with friends and family.

What might the living room or dining room represent? Think about questions you might ask pertaining to their symbolism. You can figure this out. What do you do there? How much time is spent there? Are they inviting?

Do you enjoy your time in them? What is in the attic, what part of your body does it correlate to?

Each room in the house has a significance to you. What do you do in that room? How is it used? Is it clean, messy, beautiful, plain? Ask the questions that come to mind. Your house reflects your vibration. Consider each room a different aspect of your life according to its purpose. Learn from the place in which you live.

CHAPTER 27

Recycle Your Life

My daughter is starting a business that takes plastic waste found on beaches and in the ocean, grinds it up, and makes it into beautiful and useful items. This new career move, like any transitional event in our lives, is a statement about us. The career we choose has a very symbolic meaning. Like any other symbolic event we start to decipher it by asking questions.

What is the business? Recycling. Recycling is transforming something that no longer has a use into something useful. It takes the old and transforms it into something new. This career choice may mean that she would like to transform herself. Einstein showed us that energy cannot be created or destroyed, it can only be transformed. This career choice is all about transforming useless trash into whatever you want.

My daughter wants to transform the old beliefs, thoughts, actions, behaviors, and emotions that are not serving her into beliefs, thoughts, actions, behaviors, and emotions that serve her well. She wants her life to be beautiful, helpful, useful, and new. She knows, perhaps still on an unconscious level, that it's time to let go of limiting beliefs and thoughts. She wants to stop polluting her life with mindless conditioning.

It is good to recycle, to transform your thoughts and beliefs. If you believe that you are stuck in your life and that it won't change, consider what it would be like to have a new belief. A belief that you can always change your life. You are a manipulator of energy. You can transform negative into positive. We are all Quantum Physicists. Change your thoughts and beliefs and transform your life. Feel the emotion associated with these new thoughts and beliefs. Reinvent yourself.

If you find yourself fantasizing about switching your career and have a specific alternative in mind, take some time to analyze it. What is this new career about? What makes it attractive? What does it symbolize? Do I really want that career, or do I want what it symbolizes. Do I want to be a different person?

Kylie, who has been a nurse for twenty years, has decided she would like to become a Death Doula. A Death Doula helps people who are dying, and their families, through the transition from being in the physical body to the vibrational Spiritual Body.

Kylie has been working very hard on transforming herself and seeking Truth. This career choice would reflect that she wants to transition herself to a higher place. When a person dies many believe they go to Heaven or a place of Love, Light, and Peace. Kylie wants to transcend from her fear-based ego mind to a place of Love, Light, and Peace.

The very first career path that I remember wanting was that of an archeologist. What is the symbolism here? What does an archeologist do? On a very simple physical level an archeologist digs things up. An archeologist discovers things. An archeologist investigates the past to find clues about our history. Why did I want to be an archeologist? I wanted to dig up the facts. I wanted to excavate the truth. I wanted to know where I came from, what tools were used to shape me, and how all of that has carried through to make me the person I am.

In many ways archeology symbolizes what I am doing now and what I'm asking everyone reading this book to do. I am asking you to use the symbols in your life as tools to unearth your subconscious beliefs. I'm asking you to dig into your past and look at the relics of your life, the memories, the forged beliefs, and the archaic, obsolete tools you were given as a child. You will discover how these old beliefs have affected your life's progress. Have the stories you unearthed shown you that your indoctrinated beliefs have helped you or hindered you?

Do you want to go into nursing? How do you envision your day as a nurse? What are you doing? How are others responding to you? Do you want to be a trauma nurse, in a fast-paced environment where every move you make could potentially save a life or end in death? Do you want to be a midwife, where you birth new life into the world? Do you want to be a hospice nurse, where you usher people through their transition to the next plane? Close your eyes and imagine that your patient is you as a child. Have a conversation with the child about what's wrong. Talk about how you can help. Allow the vision to go wherever it takes you. What happened? Imagine what your day would be like as a nurse. What are you doing? How does it affect others? How do you feel?

Do you want to be a lawyer? Why? For justice, prestige, money? What does a lawyer represent to you? Imagine a scene with you as a lawyer. What do you enjoy about it? How are you acting? Are you self-righteous or humble? Are you defending someone or prosecuting? Are you a constitutional or an international business lawyer? What does each type mean to you?

Do you want to be a teacher? Why? Do you want to change the system? Do you want to heal your inner child? Close your eyes and imagine you are in front of a classroom and one of the students is you as a child. They raise their hand, and you call on them. What do they say to you? How do you respond? Look out over your classroom. Do you see some children who remind you of specific times or people? Is it one of your childhood classrooms? What do you remember about that time that made you feel special or loved? Do you want to revisit that feeling in your career? Do you want to help a child the way you were helped?

Whenever you think of a career that intrigues you, try to pinpoint what it is within that career that you find especially appealing. Do you want to be a great actor or do you want to be a movie star? Do you want to be a great athlete or do you want to win a gold medal? Do you want to work in the financial sector or do you want a sailboat and a big house?

When we carefully consider the motives behind our career choices, we may see that our goal is not the career itself, but a part of it that appeals to a part of us. There are few careers that fulfill one completely. What did you do as a child that made you happy? How could that translate into a career? I loved going into the woods.

Working as a park ranger might have served me better than the unconscious choices I made.

What messages about financial security were you indoctrinated with as a child? Were you encouraged to do what you love or told to follow a practical career? DON'T DO WHAT YOU HATE! Nothing that disturbs your peace that much is worth it. If you absolutely dread going to work each morning, please spend some time questioning what would bring you joy and pursue that avenue. You deserve a life doing what you love for the simple reason that you are here. You are not here to strive and suffer. You are here to thrive and grow. *Life can be what you love or what you've been told*. Choose to live the life you love. Claim a new truth.

The Collective Consciousness can be likened to Infinity. It always has been, is now, and always will be. It has all the knowledge of everything that has ever happened and ever will happen. If everything is energy, and it is, then nothing can be destroyed, only transformed. Every thought, every idea, every event, everything is in the quantum field. With this knowledge the Collective can bring you any answer that you require to realize your goals. Why would we trust our limited knowledge of the world when the universe holds all knowledge and is just waiting for you to ask the questions? Be open to its answers. What job would bring me fulfillment? What do I like to do? What do I get excited about? What did I love to do as a kid? What is the best path for me?

Science fiction writers have often written about inventions and scientific theories that weren't even a concept in the minds of the scientists of their time and yet, the stories they write become the truth of the future. They are drawing from the timeless Collective Consciousness.

Whenever I meet someone who says they have never had an experience outside of the five senses, I ask them if they ever had the feeling that someone was staring at them when their back was turned to that person. They all have said that they have experienced that feeling. We turn and see the person looking at us. I ask the person who denies experience outside of the five senses to explain how they sensed the person staring at them. They can't explain it because it is an experience of energy. It is not an experience of touch, taste, smell, sight, or hearing. A dog can hear sounds and smell things we can't. A cat can see colors and light that we can't. This means there is more than our five senses can experience. Our mind is not our brain. It is our consciousness. It is energetic and has a frequency. Just as we use our physical senses, we can use our vibrational senses to enhance our lives.

Knowing that there is more to this world than we can sense helps us to imagine that the universe can provide us with a blessing, an answer, help to rescue us from ourselves. Be open to what your Higher Self has to offer you.

In the 1960's my mother worked in a bank and progressed to Head Teller; she hit the glass ceiling. There would be no higher position she could hold at the bank. She would never be a manager or vice president; she would never be on the board. Head Teller was it. One day a con man came in and conned her out of two hundred dollars. She had had many con artists come to her teller's window in the past and try to confuse her, but she had always caught them and alerted the authorities. This time she got fooled. The bank fired her.

She was more upset than I had ever seen her. She felt betrayed by the employers for whom she had worked honestly and hard for so many years. She was at a low point in her life.

A good friend called and told her about a job with the company she worked for. Mom applied for and got the job. It was a large company and there was plenty of room for growth. Faster than most she had a management position in the exciting new field of computer technology. She thrived in her new environment. She was intellectually stimulated and found the work fascinating. She had been afraid to leave a small secure job even though it offered her no hope for advancement and was far below her intellectual capacity. She had been devastated when she lost that job but getting fired was the best career move she ever made. Thank you, Collective Consciousness for doing what she didn't have the courage to do for herself. The Collective Consciousness gave her an opportunity for growth she would have never received had she not been fired. She accepted an opportunity even though it wasn't familiar to her. *Every bad thing that happens to us is an opportunity for growth and happiness, or bitterness and resentment.* Choose to see challenges and disappointments as Acts of Grace and look for the silver lining. *Everything is a gift.*

Is there a career that intrigues you? Do you daydream about living in a specific area? I once thought about moving to Asheville, NC. Someone told me that what I really wanted was a care-free hippie lifestyle. Asheville is known as a bit of a creative hippie haven.

I didn't need to move to Asheville, I needed to change my life.

What daydreams do you have about career, vacations, houses, location? What do they represent? I belonged to a Community Supported Agriculture program for a few years. It is a program where you buy shares in a local farm and get a weekly share of the produce. I pulled into the parking lot once and saw that every car there was a Subaru Outback. Five of them. Clearly that car represents a certain culture. What car would you choose if you could have any car at all? What does it represent? Cars are what drive us through life. Are we driven by concerns for the earth, practicality, financial status, spiritual growth? Cars are marketed to certain demographics. Remember you are a unique individual soul, not a demographic.

Our choices, whether career, car, food, shelter, or clothing, represent a part of our emotional and spiritual belief systems. What do your daydreams tell you about yourself, what do they symbolize? Consider the reasons for the choices you make. What does it represent to you?

CHAPTER 28

Driven to Greatness

There is some general symbolism that applies to almost everyone. Your car represents your path in life. Common expressions like "the highway of life" clearly point to this interpretation. Put on the brakes! He was working too hard and ran out of gas. I've been doing that for years; it's time to switch gears.

Low air in the tires might mean that your life force is low. Air represents the life force. When we breathe, inspire, we receive life. When we stop breathing, expire, we lose life. Are we living an inspired life? A dead battery; you've run out of energy or your vibration is low. In whichever part of your car you have an issue, look at what that part does to figure out the meaning in your life.

If we get stuck in the snow or mud we may ask if we are stuck in a rut in our life. Do we continue to have the same romantic relationship every time, but with a different person? Do our partners have the same behaviors or personalities; are we reacting to their behaviors in the same pattern? Did we learn this style of relationship from the relationships modeled to us as children? Do we choose people who are like our parents? Is our life monotonous? We may stay in a rut, whether bored at work or in an uninspiring lifestyle or relationship, until we learn the lesson that it offers.

There are times in everyone's life when we are propelled out of a rut and into change against our will. It may be the involuntary end of a relationship or job. Later, and sometimes it takes years, we are grateful that what seemed like a terrible loss delivered incredible new opportunities and growth. We are grateful that we stopped living a life that offered us crumbs.

If we really want to change something we need to start. Martin Luther King, Jr. said that we "don't need to see the whole staircase, just take the first step." Take the first step and trust that the next step will be revealed, trust that the people who can help you will show up when needed. Ask your Higher Self for guidance. We have help if we but ask. Get out of that rut!

If you have a dream about a car, who's in the driver's seat? Symbolically, the person driving is the active aspect, and the passenger is the passive. Let's say you dream your mother is driving the car and you are in the passenger seat. You may not consciously think you are following Mom's mandates but if she's driving the car just consider the possibility that her beliefs are steering your life. Are you functioning from a place of unconscious, conditioned Momisms? How has the person driving influenced your personal beliefs about love, money, career, and happiness? How do they model living to you? Are they a risk taker or do they follow the status quo? Consider the dominant trait of the person driving and see if that trait in you has been driving your decision-making process recently. What other traits do they have that you relate to or see in yourself?

If someone else is driving your car it may represent a co-dependent relationship. In codependent relationships one person takes all the responsibility. The other person in the relationship, in an unconscious exchange of responsibility for what they see as freedom, gives up all their power. For a while everything goes along smoothly. I'm happy, you're happy. Then, the resentments start. Responsible one resents the person who doesn't do any work, they rail and say, "I do everything around here." They do, but initially they did it because they liked all the power. What did they really get? False power, it's called control.

The "free" one resents the responsible one. It was nice to have someone else take over all the responsibilities and work, but, dammit, I want to have a say. They agreed to the nonverbal contract for a while. Now they miss having input, having a voice.

That's codependence, so if you dream that your partner is driving the car then check to see if you've made an unconscious bargain; do they run the show in exchange for taking all the responsibility. If you're driving and your partner is the passenger in a dream that may mean you have taken all the responsibility. You may also see this pattern in parent and adult child relationships, and with siblings or friends as well.

Did your parents model a codependent relationship? Did one of them run the show while the other was passive? Did they resent each other's controlling behaviors? Were you often controlled by your parents in what you consider an extreme way? Were you given the responsibility for the care of your younger siblings? Were you required to help run the household as a child? You may be continuing the role of the responsible one in relationships and choosing passive partners who enable that role.

Maggie was rear ended while at a stop sign. Because of our work together interpreting symbolism she immediately started to look for the meaning of it. What signs were there? There was literally a Stop sign! She grasped that she was at a standstill in her life. She wasn't going anywhere. She had been talking about going to nursing school for quite some time and wasn't doing anything to move forward with her goal. She realized she was getting a kick in the rear (rear end accident) to get her going in the right direction. This symbolism propelled her into action and she's now a nurse starting a new position she's very excited about. The rear end of the car also represents the past, it is what's behind you. This reinforces the collision's message that it's time to move forward and put the past behind you.

Are you having transmission trouble? Do you feel like you are stuck in first gear or careening along in overdrive. Have you been trying, but unable to get out of the current situation you find yourself in? If you consider other approaches to your issue, switch gears, you may find the answer.

Radiator trouble? This would represent the red, heat symbolism. Because a problem is a negative it could be alerting you to the negative aspects of the symbol such as anger issues or a lack of passion in your life, a lack of creative outlet, or dull relationship. Do you find yourself angry and irritable more than you'd like? Are you letting off steam? Do you have a rewarding creative outlet? Is there passion in your life, not just romantic, but in the form of a project, interest, or avocation?

Bald tires? Think about the car issue, ask what the job of that part of the car is, relate the symbolism to your life. Do you have a grip on your life or are you careening out of control? Time to get some traction going, get a firm grip on what is needed to move forward.

We need to have brake maintenance done regularly. Whenever we need our brakes done, it's a good time to put on our brakes and take stock of where we are. It's time to make sure we're not just going full speed ahead without checking in to see if we're on the right track. Do you sometimes feel like you're not living your life, not making choices, but being carried along in life's momentum? Brake time is the time to stop, take stock, and make sure we are making conscious decisions and not acting from our conditioning.

Having our oil changed is the same concept. Whenever you have it changed, look at your symbolism of it. For me, raised as Catholic, anointing of oil is done to set someone apart, to make one Holy, to clean away the negative, low energies. But I tend to look at the spiritual symbolism. Since the last oil change, I would ask if I have put focus on my spiritual growth. Am I moving towards wholeness or moving in the opposite direction? What would it mean to you? Oil eases the way for action, it is a lubricant. It helps unstick things. How might that apply? Can you think of any other purpose or symbolism for oil?

What car issues have you had lately? Do you have a recurring issue with your car? See it as a reflection of your path in life. What small adjustments can you make to get your life in gear and moving in the right direction? It's time to run on all cylinders and take the high road. That's too many metaphors.

CHAPTER 29

Stop Dogging Me!

I once had a very frightening encounter with a coyote in the woods. I was walking with my dog, Sophie, and my daughter's dog, Pico. The small dog, Pico, suddenly went on high alert and I looked in the direction he was looking. There was a coyote about 15 feet from us. Pico took a few steps toward it. When the coyote saw that I had spotted it, it bared its teeth and growled at me. I instinctively reacted by growling back as loudly as I could and called both dogs to me. The coyote backed off about 8 feet. My larger dog, Sophie, went after it. I kept Pico with me and whistled for Sophie.

I turned around and hurried Pico back down the path in the direction from which we had come. Sophie came running back right away, but so did the coyote, trailing about 15 feet behind us on the path. I kept turning around to growl at it. I had been out foraging for mushrooms at the time and had a basket and a mushroom knife with me. I would swing the basket and flash the knife at it. I did what I could to appear large and threatening to it. Though it would stop momentarily when I turned around it didn't back off. Then it started to circle around on our right in the woods stalking us. Sophie whined a few times because she wanted to go after it, but she stayed in front with Pico between us. This went on for at least five minutes, probably longer, and we were moving fast. I had to look back frequently to be sure it wasn't getting closer. It finally backed off. I'm not sure exactly when, but because it had been tracking us in the woods I kept my knife out and kept visually searching the woods all around us. I've never had that happen with coyotes before. Generally, if I see a coyote in the woods the moment it makes eye contact it runs off. Coyotes have no interest in humans and don't see us as prey.

This was very unusual behavior. Later that day I was told that it was probably a young male that had been ousted from the den, as they naturally are at that time of year, to fend for themselves. When I learned this it completely changed how I viewed the situation. I immediately knew the young coyote wasn't trying to attack us but that he was incredibly frightened upon seeing a human and two dogs, maybe for the very first time. Imagine how scary that would be. Perhaps he just wanted to make sure we were out of his territory so he would feel safe.

What did this experience mean? I was going through a very difficult time when this happened. I was having a lot of anxiety. I was very emotional. Sometimes I didn't even know why.

This coyote was mirroring my fear and anxiety. It was telling me to stop going down that path. Fear and worry belonged to him, not to me. He was aggressive because of his fear. Whenever we act from ego we are acting from fear. My energy of fear and anxiety had attracted more fear and anxiety. This seemed to be a very clear message once I got it. I was going down the path of fear and what else would I expect to meet on this path but more fear. The only thing fear does is bring us more fear, more anxiety, more doubt.

What was I afraid of? Was I afraid of others? These are the questions that need to be asked when faced with a symbol of your fears. Like the coyote, did I mistrust others and think they were out to harm me? Growing up in a family where I wasn't protected, where I often feared angry outbursts from my father, may have left me with beliefs that I can't trust those in positions of power or those who are supposed to love and protect me.

The coyote was being aggressive. He had been thrown out of his home without any support. Did I feel unsupported, alone, unable to cope by myself? Did my feelings of anxiety have to do with that? Was I attacking others? It didn't have to be externally. Was I having thoughts of blame, anger, or harsh judgment? I needed to see where I was feeling distrust and analyze what indoctrinated belief system I held. Whenever we attack others it is because we are feeling attacked. We are being defensive.

This wonderful coyote was telling me not to go down that path. Leave fear behind. Turn around and go back to a place of trust and love. What were the dogs telling me? Sophie was my dog, she wanted to chase the coyote away. She represented the part of me, the wild, intuitive me, that knew she could easily banish the fear. I held her back. I wasn't listening to my intuition at that time. The little dog listened to me and got in line to take the safe path back home.

The coyote went into the woods on my right to stalk us. The right side is the masculine side, the active side. This is telling me that I need to take action and work on my fear and anxiety, that I can't be passive and allow it to rule my life.

Within a week of this coyote experience I drove around a corner and saw the same coyote on the side of the road scavenging. I knew it was the same one because of his distinctive solid red coat. He had a piece of takeout food litter and he was trying to lick off the last bit of food, if there was any there at all.

I stopped the car, rolled the window down, and called softly to him. I wanted to get over any residual fear I might have had from the experience and, also just wanted to see what his reaction would be. He completely ignored me, not even looking up. After a couple of minutes with no response from him I drove the car around the corner and there alongside the road were three rabbits grazing on some clover. The rabbits were not fifty feet from him. He was scavenging on trash while a bountiful feast was right around the corner.

If the coyote represents part of me, it means my focus on fear driven thoughts was keeping me from seeing the abundance (rabbit symbolism) waiting for me right around the corner. If I would only believe that it was there, that I was worthy, that I deserved it, it would be mine. If I let go of the fear of lack (scavenging coyote) and know my worthiness I will be showered with abundance. Instead, I was accepting scraps. I believed that abundance wasn't for me.

The coyote reminded me that abundance is here, waiting for me to allow it into my life. The vibration of abundance is simply waiting for us to accept it. I love that message!

The biggest fears we have, fear of failure, fear of not fitting in, fear of embarrassment, fear of betrayal, fear of rejection, fear of abandonment, fear of loneliness, *fear of lack*, fear of death, fear of judgment, *fear of being unworthy and unlovable*, and fear of the loss of loved ones, all originate from the fear that "God" doesn't love us, that we are separate, that we are unworthy of Love, and that we are bad and therefore don't deserve anything good in our lives.

What is your greatest fear? Try to separate it from the conglomeration of all your fears. The fear of lack can include lack of money, lack of love, lack of relationship, lack of any kind of happiness or abundance. If you are afraid that you will miss out on some aspect of the life you have been told will bring you happiness, you have a fear of lack. Do we really want the things we are told will make us happy? *Can you separate what will make you happy from what you have been told will make you happy?* If I buy a house, I'll be happy. If I'm in a relationship, I'll be happy. If I have children, I'll be happy. All collective constructs. What do YOU want?

We will not gain joy from external sources. All the things we are told will make us happy, will not. Accepting ourselves, loving ourselves in our flawed humanity, *knowing that we are loved in our flawed humanity will bring us peace*. God is talking to you and wants you to know you are fully known and still fully loved.

Fear is how we create lack in our lives. The external fears like spiders, snakes, and coyotes are symbolic of our internal fears which represent our one real fear;

the erroneous belief that we are separate from Source and, in extension, separate from one another. This world mirrors our beliefs about who we are. When we believe in our worthiness the whole world opens before us and we can have it all. Knowing we are fully loved no matter what we've done brings us to the path of self-love. Leave the path of fear and just around the corner you will find abundance.

CHAPTER 30

They Never Leave Us

When a Loved One passes it can be overwhelming. If it's too early in your grief to read this chapter, it may be best to come back to it.

When someone we love dies, we want to know where they are, that they are safe and happy. We want them to send us a sign that they are okay and still with us. Sometimes, if they know that they are dying, Loved Ones will set up a sign to share after they pass. Signs, symbols, and synchronicities after a death are gifts from our Loved Ones.

Simon's and Beth's father always picked up pennies when he saw them on the ground and would make a comment about saving pennies. After their father's death they saw pennies on the street, on the sidewalk, in hallways. They knew their father was sending them signs that he was still with them. Ask those that have passed to send you a sign. It may be better to leave the specifics open and be completely surprised at the unique way in which you are contacted. You will know it's them.

They may visit in a dream. Interestingly when they come to me in dreams the symbolism is often that they are on vacation. They are having the time of their lives, absolutely no worries, they love it there. They can't wait to see you again in their perfect vacation getaway. But, since there is no time where they are, waiting is not a problem, they want you to live a long and joyful life.

A man I know suffered greatly from mesothelioma before he died. He couldn't do anything for himself, he was in pain, his life was a misery to him. After he passed, he came to me in a dream. He presented himself as a puppet. He then showed me all the strings being cut and the complete freedom he was experiencing, the joy of a freedom we won't know on this planet. Clearly a message that he was no longer suffering, he could do anything he pleased and was happy and at peace. I don't call myself a medium though sometimes Loved Ones show up during a reading or even out of the blue. The feeling that I get from them, the vibration, is pure Love and Joy. They are immersed in Love and Joy and they want you to know that.

Birds are often signs of Loved Ones visiting us. This makes sense to me as birds are not tied to the earth. They are symbolically in a higher realm, free of earthly limitations. Butterflies and dragon flies hold this symbolism as well. If you are outside and ask for a sign you may have a bird show up and do something to make you take notice.

Pets will send us messages as well. After my daughter's beagle, Bailey, passed I heard the familiar tinkle of dog tags where she had walked along beside me. Years ago, I was doing a card reading for a woman and she wanted to ask a question without saying it out loud. Instantly I had a vision of two dogs in a sporty convertible. They were ready to go for a drive. The male dog was in the driver's seat, he was wearing a dashing cap, sunglasses, and scarf. The female dog in the passenger seat was wearing a lovely polka dot scarf and sunglasses, very glamorous. They were decked out. I almost didn't tell the woman what I was seeing. It seemed too fanciful and didn't make sense to me, but I decided to plunge in. She said if I hadn't told her about my vision she wouldn't have believed a word of the whole reading. When the dogs were alive, every week she and her son dressed them up and took them for a Sunday drive. The dogs were letting her know they were still enjoying their fancy dress Sunday drives and thanking her for such a good life.

The first time I ever channeled was with friends. We decided to have a mediumship evening. I closed my eyes and saw a couple standing in front of some very dense woods on the far side of a body of water. Often a body of water between you signifies they have crossed over. I told one of my friends that I thought the message was for her and described the physical attributes of the couple. She said it sounded like her aunt and uncle. Their message to her was that even though they fought like cats and dogs while on earth they were extremely happy now and in a place of Love. She said they fought constantly. I kept stressing that the woods meant something, but she couldn't figure it out. Finally, it clicked, and she told me their last name was Forest.

About twenty years ago I was working as a nurse in a long-term care facility. One morning in November after I arrived at work I was overcome with sadness. I thought I might start sobbing. I was having a hard time holding my composure. I didn't know what was causing my heightened emotion. There was a patient on the unit who had severe dementia. She was confined to a wheelchair, immobile, nonverbal, and completely dependent on staff for all her needs. Yet, there she was, using her hands to turn the wheels and move her chair. I had worked with her for over a year and never seen her move. The other nurses started to comment on it. We were all shocked. She wheeled over to me and was staying by my side as I moved down the hallway with the med cart. I continued my rounds and the overwhelming sadness stayed with me. She stayed beside me in her wheelchair. I suddenly remembered it was the first anniversary of my older brother's death. Here was the cause of my sadness. Just as I realized it, she looked up at me and said, "There's someone here. Oh! It's your mother!" and she blew me a kiss. My mother passed two years before my brother. An elderly woman with advanced dementia gave me a message from her. We never know how our Loved Ones may contact us.

The only reason I believe a Loved One won't contact us after they die is if there is a soul contract that doesn't allow it. This happened to me. We may need to experience our emotions and realize our strength. We may need to learn independence. We may need to learn to appreciate and be grateful for the family and friends that we still have on this physical plane. Though it may never be clear what the reason for their silence is, everything happens in Divine Order. Any challenge we face is a call for growth.

Often language doesn't come into play when interpreting messages from Loved Ones. A rose may signify an anniversary. A candle may be the symbol for a birthday. A ring may symbolize a wedding. If you are thinking of a Loved One who passed and get a vision of something, think about what it means to you. What does it make you think of? How could it be connected to them? Is it something you shared? If nothing comes to mind right away, let it sit for a while and simmer. The answer will come. And you'll probably laugh, or cry.

Sometimes our Loved Ones clearly display their humor in messages. I was doing a card reading for a woman; it was the first anniversary of her eighteen-year-old son's death. I envisioned him laughing and he showed me snakes. She had a snake phobia and he used to prank her by leaving rubber snakes around, having a good laugh at her reactions. This is an evidential reading. There is no way I could have known that. When she first arrived, she told me about her son and how upset she was that not one person had called her to acknowledge the day. People want to talk about their loved ones who have passed. Let them share with you. Be a loving listener.

An early death, especially the death of a child, may render someone unable to cope. They may need constant support. This is understandable. Signs from their child will help. If we aren't receiving any messages, it may be that we are too grief stricken to recognize the messages and so the Loved One comes to us through someone else. Don't take it personally if you don't receive messages. There are reasons for everything. Continue to ask and when you are ready the signs will come directly to you.

There is nothing easy about someone we love passing. Please try to remember that they haven't left us, they are just in a different form. You can't touch them or see them, but they are with you. If you are overwhelmed with grief, having a hard time functioning, or falling into depression, visit a reputable medium. Try to get referrals. A good medium will give you an evidential message. The message will be about something that they couldn't possibly know. They can act as conduits until we can see for ourselves the loving messages being sent.

After my younger brother died his wife was inconsolable. He gave me a message about their dog, Popcorn. He called Popcorn the daughter they never had. He wanted me to tell his wife that. When I did, she smiled and said that's what they used to call her. It was their private joke. Having evidential signs is a wonderful way to validate messages from our Loved Ones.

A woman who was going to do psychic/mediumship readings for the first time was nervous and wanted to do a "practice" reading for me before she started. She told me that my best friend who had passed was laughing and saying to not drink distilled water, that I needed the minerals in tap water. I have a thing about water that only my family and close friends know about. There was no way the medium could have known this. My daughter got a reading from her that day and was highly impressed with the things she told her that she couldn't have known.

When tragedy strikes it may be impossible to consider that some good may come of it. When we feel broken and are despairing it's hard to see a hint of light. As time goes by, we may notice that we are seeing a particular animal or bird frequently, we are hearing a particular song on the radio quite often, or hearing and reading words that have special meaning. A stranger may say something that reminds you of them. Take these signs to heart. Notice the synchronicities. Let them inform you that you are loved, you are not forgotten and never will be.

Never blame yourself for the death of someone you love, even if you feel you were responsible for them. We often think we could have done more, or we somehow contributed to them dying sooner, or we weren't there for them. Don't punish yourself. We all come into this world with a purpose, a plan specifically for this lifetime. Some people come into our lives as angels to leave us earlier than we expected. It's not an easy task being the one to cause pain in a soul group but they help us to realize there has to be a better way. They help us realize that we don't want a life of suffering. We've had enough. This is their gift. It leads us to stop trying to experience peace from an ego driven life. The time to allow the Source of Love to enter our lives, to guide us, to bring us peace has arrived. We can't change what has happened, but we can try to bring the Highest Good that can come from it. Perhaps it's a closer relationship with the ones who share our loss, the others who were left behind. Perhaps it's a closer relationship with our Higher Self, our True Self. Perhaps it's a greater appreciation and gratitude for life in general.

Our Loved Ones move to another dimension before us as part of our Soul Group's plan. Please don't ever think that death is a punishment, that it is cruel and unfair. There is a bigger plan, a mystery, and we will know the reason for it all when we eventually join them in the same form, in that better place. Until then, know they are with you now and always.

CHAPTER 31

Using Symbols in Guided Meditation

Consciously using symbolism can bring us some startling results. Guided meditations are one of the best ways to do this.

For example, we can use a guided meditation to answer a question we've been contemplating. Before delving into the symbolism of the following guided meditation I'd like you to do the meditation. After reading the following meditation, think of a question, close your eyes, and imagine this story.

You are walking along the right side of a river. To your right is your first home, your first family is there with you, you see everyone interacting as they do. They go inside and you imagine all of you watching TV in the evening or you in your room on the computer or phone if that was part of your childhood. You pass the schools you attended and see the kids you grew up with. You pass churches or other religious buildings that gave you some of your beliefs. You pass your current home, workplace or school, people, and surroundings. You see them all but make no judgment. You pass a lovely meadow. You take a deep breath and let out a relaxing sigh. On the left is a walking bridge crossing the river.

As you cross the bridge you look over the railing and you see the river flowing along. You can spend some time here if you wish. On the other side of the river are deep woods with a path that leads into them. You take this path. It is cool and shadowy but rays of sunlight through the leaves dapple the ground. It is quite lovely and relaxing.

You may see strangers or animals on this path. Stop and talk with them if it feels right. You may see someone you know or who has passed on. They may just say hello, give you a hug, or they may have something important to tell you. Take time with them if you need to, there's no hurry.

A little farther down the path you come to a bright clearing. In the middle of the clearing is a cottage surrounded by vibrantly blooming flowers and a fence. There is a fruit tree on either side of the walkway. You open the front gate knowing you are expected. You know that something very wise and wonderful is going to be shown to you. You close the gate behind you and walk to the front door. You knock and the door is opened. The person, animal, or entity opening the door may be someone you know or not. They are thrilled to see you and invite you in. You feel very comfortable with them and know that they are here specifically to help you. They love you and want you to be happy.

There is a table with two chairs in front of a fireplace with a warming fire. The table is set with two cups. You both sit down at the table. You tell your host how happy you are to be there and they thank you for coming. Your host pours your favorite hot drink into each cup. You feel like you are home and you both sit quietly for a bit in comfortable silence enjoying your drink.

When it feels right you ask your question. The answer will be instantaneous. If the answer sounds confusing it may be symbolic, but usually the answers are quite clear. After you have done this guided meditation read on to see the symbolism of this story.

Why does this meditation work? What is the symbolism behind it? You are walking along a river, a river leads to the ocean, which is symbolic of your path to reclaim your Divine Self. Remembering who you are is the purpose of your life's journey.

On the right side of the river are representations of your early life. It is the physical realm, the ego world in which you have chosen to live, and which has programmed you to accept a certain paradigm. You see your family, religious center, and schools, which represent your childhood. This is where you learned most of your unconscious beliefs about yourself. Then you see your current life. This is what you have created with those beliefs.

Next you experience a space of relaxation, a tranquil meadow, before you cross the bridge. You cross from the right side, the masculine side of action and doing, to the left side, the feminine side of nurturing and receiving (open to the answer to your question).

The landscape on the other side of the river is quite different. There is nothing there of your life. You enter a new path. Where you are going is unclear (the question). You have left behind your beliefs and your familiar life.

You come out of the woods. The sun breaks through (a light that reveals all). This is the place where everything is made clear (a clearing). You see a cottage surrounded by a fence, this is a safe place for you. There are fruit trees. Your journey will bear fruit. There are flowers blooming, your consciousness is blossoming.

You knock on the door and it is opened. Here before you is the being who knows the answers to all of your questions and is inviting you in to this place of the One Consciousness. You sit in front of a fire with them. Fire is purifying, cleansing, and creative. It burns away your doubts and fears. You have your drink. The cup represents the Holy Grail, the Divine Knowing, the Embodiment of the Christ Consciousness. As you drink from the cup you are accepting Divine Knowing. The cup also symbolizes the feminine aspects of allowing and receiving. It represents your openness to the answer you will receive. You ask your question and you get your answer (ask and it is given).

Sometimes people doing this meditation meet loved ones or guides on the path to the cottage. Did you meet anyone on the path? What did they have to say to you? Was it a cathartic experience? Often unresolved familial issues are resolved through this meditation. I met my deceased mother on the path once and she spoke to me words that helped heal my heart.

You can also use this meditation to consciously speak with those with whom you need to have closure, those with whom you still share an unresolved painful history, whether they are still here or have passed over you can speak with them. Go to the cottage, they will answer the door and when it's time you can ask them questions or just tell them how you feel. They will respond with just what you need to hear.

Develop a meditation that brings you peace. There may be someone you miss and you just want to see them and talk with them. Have them answer the door. Put in aspects of your life that have meaning to you. Add side paths if you are trying to make a choice. Which path brings you happiness? You can make up your own visualizations spontaneously by just closing your eyes and beginning your walk along the river. See what happens. Remember the images and see what the symbolism is on your adventure in imagination. You may be surprised at the amazing places you take yourself. You have unlimited options. You are an unlimited creative being.

CHAPTER 32

Symbols of the Collective

During the evolution of humans there have always been collective symbols. Some remain the same, the archetypal symbols, and some change or are added as humans evolve. These symbols form an insight into the beliefs of the culture. As media infiltrates virtually every place on earth we become more homogenous in the meaning of our collective symbols.

During the early twentieth century Carl Jung introduced the idea of archetypes, symbols, and the collective consciousness. He was a brilliant man who knew that our minds are not the same as our brains. Our mind enables us to recognize that our thoughts are not necessarily our own, but merely echoes of our past programming. He proposed that our Consciousness was the part of our mind that witnessed our thoughts and, hopefully, questioned them. Have you heard the quote from Allan Lokos, "Don't believe everything you think?" Thoughts jump into our heads all the time, often in the form of reactionary assumptions, conditioned responses, and always as *vibrational matches* to our frequency. Our unconscious thoughts are almost exclusively triggered by emotions. Regardless, we don't choose our thoughts. We can decide to think about something that we need to do, but the thoughts that come are programmed. We don't think our thoughts, they are conditioned reactions to past experiences.

Jung advised us to delve into our belief systems, to broaden our concept of who we are. He believed that we are living multiple realities and that we are just beginning to see the infinite quality of our consciousness. He interpreted the symbols and synchronicities in his life almost constantly as an experiment in exploring the depths of the human psyche.

Let's explore shared consciousness. Consider what is known as the One Hundredth Monkey Effect. On an island off Japan live Macaque monkeys. In 1952 scientists were studying these primates whose main food source is sweet potatoes. One day an adolescent female took a dirty, sandy sweet potatoes to the river and washed it, making it much more palatable. As other monkeys watched her, they began to imitate her example and washed their sweet potatoes as well. After a time, monkeys on the island who hadn't witnessed potato washing started to rinse off their sweet potatoes. Then an extraordinary event occurred, monkeys on a nearby island who couldn't have seen any other monkeys washing sweet potatoes started washing their sweet potatoes. This is a prime example of the shared consciousness. The minds of the Macaque monkeys were connected in the shared consciousness. Our energy, thoughts, beliefs, ideas, creations, and the Truth are all connected in our Universal Consciousness.

Another example of the Universal Consciousness is the proliferation of inventors inventing the same devices at the same time. While Alexander Graham Bell was inventing the telephone in America, a Frenchman, George Bourseul, a telegraph operator, put forward the idea of a telephone, and in Germany Philip Reis is known to have invented the telephone. Every thought ever thought, every idea ever sparked, every creation ever imagined is in the Universal Consciousness.

If we are open, we can imagine anything because it is all in the Universal Consciousness. You might think of it as an archive of everything past, present, and future. Some call it the Akashic Records. We can draw any answers we need from the Universal Consciousness. Look at science fiction authors who predicted nuclear power, escalators, video chatting, cell phones, ear buds, androids, spaceships, and nuclear submarines. Using the theory of relativity, we can understand that they tapped into the Universal Consciousness to receive their ideas from so called future events. The Universal Consciousness is timeless and holds every idea ever conceived, and in a linear sense it holds every idea that will be conceived.

"The lyrics, the strings, the chords, everything comes at the moment like a gift that is put right into your head and that's how I hear it," said Michael Jackson during the 'Dangerous' court case of 1994." From *The Incredible Way Michael Jackson Writes Songs* by Lucy Jones 08/29/2018.

Michael Jackson knew that his creativity was in the collective, he was open to receiving inspiration. He once commented that he had to get a new song produced before Prince got it. He believed that the song was there for the receiving and he was afraid Prince might download it from the Collective Consciousness first. Bob Dylan is credited with saying that all his songs were divinely inspired and that he couldn't write those songs if he tried. When we are open to inspiration amazing things can happen.

Let's see what creative symbols our current society and shared consciousness has come up with. First, we'll look at the icons of the very recent past and the present. Who hasn't heard of zombies?

There is a plethora of zombie movies, books, graphic novels, and TV shows available now. What do zombies represent? Let's look at just one example of the iconography of zombies. Arguably the most popular zombie story, from the graphic novel and TV series, is *The Walking Dead*. We are taken to a dystopian future where a virus causes people to become zombies when they die. These zombies walk together in "herds." Their only drive is to eat living beings.

Zombies are a fearful lot. They are decaying humans. They are grotesque and there is no reasoning with a zombie.

Zombies represent those who blindly follow the leader, people who don't question the status quo or reason things out. One example is those raised to believe in racism who never question the validity of their belief. They blindly follow the paradigm of superiority they were taught as children. Some people follow a political party or a religion without questioning any of the tenets of those organizations, often because their parents belonged to that political party or faith. Zombies represent any group that follows the consensus, the social paradigms, and the accepted norm without recognizing or questioning their option to make a conscious choice. They have no conscious mind. They are completely enslaved by their conditioning.

Look at history to give us examples. Slavery was once considered morally acceptable, it was legal. The Crusades, which tortured and murdered over a million people was sanctioned by a church. Millions of Jews were murdered prior to and during World War II and it was authorized by a government. These atrocities were committed by people who didn't question the authority that told them their actions were righteous. They were virtual zombies.

I once asked someone if they believed in God. He said that he did and when I asked why he responded that it was what he was taught as a child. He had never questioned one of the most important decisions of his life, whether we are alone in this universe, if there is a greater power, or if there is another alternative entirely.

What are we doing today that is considered acceptable, standard practice and/or legal that will be seen as barbaric, or elitist years from now? What are we doing now that takes away the rights of some people because they don't share the same beliefs as the majority? How are we masking a major cultural/economic/social agenda and normalizing it at the expense of certain groups?

The zombies represent humans who are not self-aware, who are not conscious. The following quote from

Paramahansa Yogananda summarizes the symbolism of zombies.

"Millions of people never analyze themselves. Mentally they are mechanical products of the factory of their environment, preoccupied with breakfast, lunch, and dinner, working and sleeping, and going here and there to be entertained. They don't know what or why they are seeking, nor why they never realize complete happiness and lasting satisfaction. By evading self-analysis, people go on being robots, conditioned by their environment. True self-analysis is the greatest art of progress."

In the story *The Walking Dead* some of the human characters start out believing they must kill other living humans to survive. No one trusts anyone. They form small bands or larger enclaves and kill not only zombies, but everyone who happens by because they are threatened and fearful of everyone but their own group. Compare this to ethnic cleansing, racial demonizing, religious superiority, political affiliation, poverty shaming, gender bias, obesity prejudice, and other ways in which exclusionary groups show their superiority and elitism.

As *The Walking Dead* progresses some of the main characters realize that they must form community and start to trust others. They recognize that their need for trust, integrity, compassion, justice, love, peace, and unity are the only things worth living for. They comprehend that a life lived in fear isn't worth living. They persuade other groups to join with them; that it is best for them to come together, best for their physical survival, but more importantly, for their peace of mind, their emotional need for community and connection, and their overall quality of life. These humans have risen above zombie mentality to a level of conscious heart guidance that will eventually bring them to the realization of Oneness.

Another significant icon of these times is that of computers. The symbolism here is much simpler. Computers are programmed. We are all programmed as children and throughout our lives. If we don't start to question our programming at an early age we will continue on an unconscious programmed path. Until we start to recognize our indoctrinated beliefs about ourselves and society and make conscious choices concerning our beliefs we will be nothing more than a computer performing its programming, Yogananda's robot.

The other interesting symbolic point about computers is that people are in front of social media for extended periods of time. It feeds the brain with Dopamine when someone *likes* our Facebook, Twitter, TikTok, or Instagram post. We are becoming addicted to social media. Rewarding us by triggering our dopamine brain receptors with "likes" is a behavioral way of programming people to return to social media platforms. *The ultimate irony is that the computer is now programming us.* We are spending more time on social media then we are spending with our friends and family. This Dopamine reward keeps us entrenched in a social programming experiment. Get into nature and recharge your natural vibrational frequency. Closing the laptop and connecting with people is healthier.

As we try to understand our core birth family programming, let's also be aware of our current societal programming through "social" and "news" media platforms and TV. Question everything!

Another way computers are a symbol of our lives is through algorithms. In the same way that computer advertising and social media is set up so that you get substance in your feed that matches your interests, searches, and with Big Brother, even your conversations, in our lives we have a *vibrational algorithm*. Our vibrational algorithm, our frequency, attracts substance in vibrational accord with us. We get back thoughts, people, things, experiences that match our vibrational frequency. I believe this is one of the simplest ways to understand the Law of Attraction.

Another prevalent emblem of our time is Artificial Intelligence, specifically androids. This is another image that is fodder for movies, books, and TV shows. In most of these stories the android comes to realize its beingness. First it questions itself. Is this all there is? Am I nothing but a computer-generated personality? Will I never be more than my programming? This self-questioning is representative of humans questioning their own lives. It is what happens when we question our unconscious beliefs, the part of us that was conditioned. In the usual narrative the android no longer blindly follows its programming but begins to accept itself as conscious; a thoughtful and feeling being with a soul, no different from any other being with a soul. The Android awakens and discards its programming to live an authentic, independent, thoughtful life.

This beautiful imagery signifies humans coming to the realization that they are more than their programming, more than their conditioned mind. It is the story of humans becoming aware of what they really are. We are Divine Beings capable of realizing Infinite and

Eternal Truth. We can now leave behind our erroneous programmed beliefs about ourselves and our collective beliefs about needing to fit into society. As more people awaken and raise their frequency it will transmit out to others and more will be awakened. This is something that each of us can do to help raise the vibration of everyone on earth. It is time for this great awakening.

There is another story line represented in the android symbolism. In the alternate story line, the android becomes aware of its ability to think on its own and starts to make independent decisions. It realizes its autonomy and uses its newly discovered power to subdue and subject humans because it fears for its survival. It thinks it must control humans to be safe. It believes humans will destroy the planet or destroy them. Their motivation is based in fear, rather than love.

In the first scenario the android becomes the Divine, in the second the android becomes the ego. We need to decide what we want for ourselves, our children, and the future generations as humanity evolves. Do we want to continue a path based in fear and separation or based in Love and Connection?

The symbolism of our society gives me great hope that we are closer to a time when all humans realize our Oneness. *Our purpose on this planet, in this realm, is to awaken humanity to its Divinity.*

Namaste is a popular cultural catch phrase. It has become so popular that many use it in an offhand manner of greeting, not knowing its true essence. The literal translation is, "I bow to you." Bowing is symbolic of humility. As defined by Mahatma Gandhi, Namaste means: "I honor the place within you where the entire Universe resides; I honor the place within you of Love, of Light, of Truth, of Peace; I honor the place within you, where, when you are in that place in you, and I am in that place in me, there is only One of us." This is a statement of humility. No one is above or below you; no one deserves more or less than you; everyone is you. This is humbling, but it is not humbling in a small or meek way. It is humbling in its enormity.

When we say Namaste with the true intention of its meaning it eventually becomes an energetic expression not requiring any thought. It is simply recognition of the Truth of our collective selves, our Oneness. Namaste is an experiential process that others can't comprehend if their belief system is still based in the five senses and the fearful realm of comparison and competition. More people are waking up. We are living beyond the five senses. We are living in Love and Oneness.

When we know how powerful our vibration is we can manifest anything. Jesus was asked by his disciples how it was that he was able to perform healing and other miracles. He told them that they could do everything he did and more. We are limitless beings hindered only by our erroneous, internalized, limiting beliefs.

Begin to see how the symbolism in your life is telling you to release the past and reach higher, to expand your understanding of what you are and of what you are capable. You are infinite. You are magnificent and wholly loved. You are as eternal as God, the Source Energy from which you were birthed.

CHAPTER 33

And In the End

The first step in interpreting your life is to notice the signs, symbols, and synchronicities that are presented to you. You may have realized that since you started reading this book you've noticed more symbols than you ever have. You may be having more vivid dreams and remembering them better. This is the reticular activator, a part of the brain designed to notice things that are forefront in your mind. When someone buys a new car they may suddenly see that model everywhere. When someone reads a book on symbolism they start seeing symbols everywhere. They are just noticing them more. That is the physical reason.

On the energetic side, when we are vibrating at a specific frequency we attract other thoughts, ideas, and external matches to our frequency. If we are thinking about signs, symbols, and synchronicities a lot we are vibrating at that frequency and will start attracting them in our life. We attract what is in the same vibration as our thoughts, emotions, and beliefs.

When you notice these symbols start to ask questions. What is the first thing that comes to mind? What does this mean to me? What do I think of when I think of him, her, it? How does it make me feel? Does it make me feel anxious, happy, or is it neutral? What does it do? What traits does it have that I share? Is it a negative or positive event, dream, symbol? Have I ever had an experience that this object, animal, or person played a significant role in? What is the most distinctive personality trait that comes to mind when thinking of this person? Questions will arise. Can you think of any other pertinent questions? You will think of them when the opportunity arises.

Don't be disappointed if you don't get answers immediately. I sometimes have the "Aha" moment days after I initially ask the questions, or even years. Divine order gives us the answers at the best possible time for us, just as the signs, symbols, and synchronicities happen when we need them most.

When memories come back to you seemingly out of the blue, be sure to question them as well. Your life reflects where you are on your journey. When you are veering off course in a direction that will make you unhappy, repeat a destructive pattern, or cause yourself and others pain, the Universe steps in to help. The Universe sends you a sign so you can turn it into an opportunity that promotes personal growth and increases your self-love and love for others.

I was fired once and within half an hour I was walking in the woods shouting, "I'm free! This is an act of Grace!" I believed that I was fired for my own good, not by my boss, but by my Higher Self, the One Consciousness. I went forward doing what I wanted, following my dreams, and it has led me to such a beautiful place. The Universe favors the courageous. Do what you love! *Everything is a gift.*

When we leave a destructive relationship, the Universe rewards us. The breakup may seem like a disaster, but it's not. We can decide how we are going to respond to any perceived challenges we face. We can make a choice to use them as an opportunity to be who we want to be, to follow our dreams, to expand our horizons, to be limitless, or we can perceive ourselves as a victim. Our beliefs make our lives.

Einstein is attributed with saying that the most important question we can ask ourselves is whether the Universe is a friendly place. I believe it's a friendly place, trying to give us direction to bring us to a purposeful joyous life. When we are in victim mentality, we see the Universe as being unfair. The Universe is never unfair. That's why the Universe sends us messages in the form of signs, symbols, and synchronicities, to wake us up to our missteps, to guide us to happiness. The Universe is trying to help us, but if we are in victim mode we can't see the opportunities, we only see the obstacles. See the friendliness of God.

You are loved beyond measure. You are always loved. It is this Love that sends you the messages. They are sent to give you guidance and inspiration because you are so very loved, and God wants you to be happy. Your happiness is the most important thing in the world. Know you are loved and love others. True Peace comes from knowing that only Love matters, only Love is real. We don't need signs, symbols, and synchronicities to know that, but they can be a welcome reminder.

CHAPTER 34

Beyond the End

Whatever happened to the disembodied voice? When I finished this book, I finally asked the question, "Who are you?" And I got an answer immediately. He told me he was one of my guides. At that moment I felt a highly intense vibration throughout my body. It was a bit unexpected and frankly, scary. Then a feminine presence came through. I had the same experience of vibration, but only on the left side, the feminine side, of my body. I knew this was to show me that though the voice I heard was masculine, the entity was completely balanced, without gender. The balance of the yin/yang, the masculine/feminine is one of the most important lessons for us. I love how they use symbols, the universal language.

I wondered how I could know all this was true and without a beat the answer, "You will know them by their fruits," came into my mind. I was unsure of the origin, so once again I googled the phrase given to me. They don't have to tell me twice! It is from Matthew 7:15-20; "Beware of false prophets, who come to you in sheep's clothing, but inwardly they are ravenous wolves. You will know them by their fruits. Do men gather grapes from thornbushes or figs from thistles? Even so, every good tree bears good fruit, but a bad tree bears bad fruit. A good tree cannot bear bad fruit, nor can a bad tree bear good fruit. Every tree that does not bear good fruit is cut down and thrown into the fire. Therefore, by their fruits you will know them."

Could my guides have given me better evidence that they are real? They are not false prophets coming to mislead me, they are my Holy Guides here to help me, bringing me full circle back to the Golden Chain tree that they insisted I google. A tree that bore this book. For me it has been very good fruit indeed. I am filled with gratitude for their presence and their constant help in creating this book. This experience has been a blessing to me. May our lives be a blessing to All That Is.

Namaste.

*"Until you make the unconscious conscious,
it will rule your life and you will call it Fate."*

—CARL JUNG

About the Author

Karen Tysver lives in a small town on the coast of New England where she writes, paints, and holds energy healing, meditation, and spiritual awakening workshops and retreats, as well as maintaining a private spiritual counseling and energy healing practice.